ZAGATSURVEY®

2000

HAWAII
TOP RESTAURANTS

Edited by Jeanette Foster

Coordinated by John McDermott

Published and distributed by
ZAGAT SURVEY, LLC
4 Columbus Circle
New York, New York 10019
Tel: 212 977 6000
E-mail: zagat@zagatsurvey.com
Web site: www.zagat.com

Acknowledgments

The Hawaiian phrase *mahalo nui loa* means thank you with heartfelt gratitude. At the top of our *mahalo nui loa* list are our surveyors who are really responsible for the success of our guide.

The impressive *Survey* response was due to the assistance of Geri Cardoza at *Pacific Business News*, Anastasy Tyran of *Gusto* magazine, and Hannah Sirois of Pacific Ocean Properties, Inc. on Kauai, wine merchants Lyle Fujioka and Richard Fields and Foodland Supermarkets on Oahu, and Harland Hughes of Connoisseur Food and Wine on Maui.

Valuable restaurant input was contributed by Lyman Blank, Bill and Patti Cook, Dennis and Susie Fitzgerald, Julia Ing, Dr. Philip and Carol McNamee, Janny Pastore, Jack and Marsha Stern, Dr. Edward and Carol Weldon, and John Tonner on Maui.

Collecting data from restaurants was done primarily by Sue McCabe, Jack Ercanbrack and Mary Adler on Oahu, Alex Sirois on Kauai, Linda Mather Olds on Maui, and Roberta Nelson on the Big Island.

We'd also like to express our appreciation to the following people who have been instrumental in letting us know of new developments in the Hawaii restaurant scene: Ruth Ann Becker, Tani Bova, Keli'i Brown, Berni Caslim-Polanzi, Gail Chew, Nancy Daniels, Sonja Fex-Rojo, Bonnie Friedman, Robin Jumper, Donna Jung, Yvonne Landavazo, Bunny Look, Joyce Matsumoto, Kimberly Mikami Svetin, Sharon Murotsune, Sweetie Nelson, Lynn Nishikawa, Alexandra Pangas, Margy Parker, Carry Porter, Kammy Purdy, Stephanie Reid, Lorne Richmond, Tom Risko, Sharon Sakai, Susan Sunderland, Gigi Valley, Caroline Witherspoon and Sandi Yara.

Contents

Starters

Here are the results of our *2000 Hawaii Top Restaurants Survey* covering nearly 400 restaurants on the Big Island of Hawaii, Kauai, Lanai, Maui, Molokai and Oahu.

By regularly surveying large numbers of local restaurant-goers, we think we have achieved a uniquely current and reliable guide. We hope you agree. More than 1,600 people participated. Since the participants dined out an average of 3.15 times per week, this *Survey* is based on about 270,000 meals per year.

We want to thank each of our participants. They are a widely diverse group in all respects but one – they are food lovers all. This book is really "theirs."

Of the surveyors, 49% are women, 51% are men; the breakdown by age is 7% in their 20s, 23% in their 30s, 31% in their 40s, 26% in their 50s and 13% in their 60s or above.

To help guide our readers to Hawaii's best meals and best buys, we have prepared a number of lists. See, for example, Hawaii's Most Popular Restaurants (page 13), Top Ratings (pages 14–17) and Best Buys (page 18). On the assumption that most people want a quick fix on the places at which they are considering eating, we have tried to be concise and to provide handy indexes.

We are particularly grateful to our editor, Jeanette Foster, the author of more than a dozen books on travel to Hawaii for Frommer's Travel Guides and a contributing writer to numerous travel magazines, and to our coordinator, John McDermott, a longtime writer on the Hawaii travel scene having written together with his late, faithful Lady Navigator, Bobbye Lee Hughes, 10 travel experience books. Along with many travel publication articles, McDermott writes a weekly travel column for *Pacific Business News*.

We invite you to be a reviewer in our next *Survey*. To do so, simply send a stamped, self-addressed, business-size envelope to ZAGAT SURVEY, 4 Columbus Circle, New York, NY 10019, or e-mail us at hawaii@zagat.com, so that we will be able to contact you. Each participant will receive a free copy of the next *Hawaii Top Restaurants Survey* when it is published.

Your comments, suggestions and even criticisms of this *Survey* are also solicited. There is always room for improvement with your help.

New York, New York
April 11, 2000

Nina + Tim
Nina and Tim Zagat

What's New

In keeping with the spirit of conciseness that characterizes Zagat reviews, we are pleased to announce that this *2000 Survey* is our most compact compilation to date, culling the islands' most important establishments (from the humble to the haute) to come up with *Hawaii Top Restaurants*. While we've streamlined the *Survey* so that it's more efficient and user-friendly, this region has been beefing up its dining scene. Here's what's happening:

The Rise of the Neighbor Islands: Once upon a time, the island of Oahu was the center of the Hawaiian culinary universe and the other islands were mere satellites, with only the occasional resort dining room or well-loved local institution to break the monotony. This pattern began to change a little more than a decade ago, when cutting-edge spots sprouted on the Big Island, Kauai, Lanai and Maui and shows no sign of abating: this year's Top 20 Food ranking boasts 14 restaurants located off Oahu.

Chefs in the News: Local superstar Alan Wong unveiled two new eateries in the past year, both audaciously set in an Oahu department store. First came the Pineapple Room, an immediate hit that he followed up with the Hawaii Regional Cuisine Marketplace, a showcase of the state's finest produce and seafood in a setting that's part deli and part grocery store. Another star, David Paul Johnson, left his renowned David Paul's Diamond Head Grill in Waikiki, which is now in the able hands of David Reardon and simply known as the Diamond Head Grill. Meanwhile on Maui, the young entrepreneurs who created the Old Lahaina Luau are not resting on their laurels, teaming with chef James McDonald (i'o, pacific'O) to produce The Feast at Lele, an upscale alfresco dining experience featuring top Pacific cuisine and extraordinary entertainment that redefines the art of the luau.

Comeback Kids: Two well-known and well-loved restaurants are back on the scene: The Willows, which for generations was *the* site for special-occasion celebrations, has reopened at the same tropical garden location in the McCully section of Oahu, and on the Big Island, the Palm Cafe returned to Alii Drive with Kevin Nutt (ex Cafe Pesto) in the kitchen.

The Future: Eight local chefs have joined forces to ensure that Hawaii's contemporary cuisine continues to flourish. The toques – Chai Chaowasaree (Chai's Island Bistro, Singha Thai), Hiroshi Fukui (L'Uraku), Beverly Gannon (Haliimaile General Store, Joe's Bar & Grill), Edwin Goto (Manele Bay, Ihilani), Jacqueline Lau (Roy's Waikoloa Bar & Grill) and James McDonald (The Feast at Lele, i'o and pacific'O) – have formed the Hawaiian Island Chefs, whose mission is to encourage, mentor and promote the next generation of island cooks by championing culinary programs at Hawaii's community colleges.

Pricing and glossary: The average cost of a meal at the restaurants contained herein is a rather reasonable $25.19. For readers unfamiliar with some of the Hawaiian and Japanese food-related terms in this book, we offer the following brief glossary:

ahi: yellowfin tuna

aku: skipjack tuna

bento: boxed meal, usually for lunch

grinds: food

hapuupuu: sea bass

haupia: coconut pudding

imu: underground oven

kaiseki: elaborate Japanese tasting menu

kajiki: Pacific blue marlin

kalua pork: pork cooked in an underground oven

kau kau: food

kiawe-grilled: grilled over aromatic, mesquite-like wood

kulolo: steamed pudding of coconut, brown sugar and taro

laulau: pork, beef or fish steamed in ti leaves

lilikoi: passion fruit

lomi salmon: salted salmon with onions and tomatoes

lumpia: Philippine egg roll

malasada: Portuguese doughnut

manapua: savory stuffed buns

manju: sweet cake with black bean filling

ohelo: berry eaten raw or cooked

okazu-ya: Japanese deli

ono: good

opakapaka: pink snapper

paniolo: Hawaiian cowboy

pau hana: after work

pipi kaula: beef jerky

plate lunch: two scoops of rice and macaroni salad served with fried fish, beef or chicken

poi: taro served pounded in a liquid form

poke: cubed raw fish with onions and seaweed served as an appetizer

pupu: appetizer

saimin: a thin broth with noodles, vegetables and fish, chicken, or pork

shave ice: snow cone

squid luau: octopus cooked in coconut milk and taro tops

taro: edible starchy root, similar to potato

teppanyaki: grilled at the table

ti: leaf used in cooking, serving and decorating

yakiniku: cook your own

We hope this *Survey* will guide you to some great gastronomic adventures. *Kahea 'ai* (come eat)!

Kailua-Kona, Hawaii
April 11, 2000

Jeanette Foster

Dining Tips

Over our 20-plus years of surveying restaurant-goers, we've heard from hundreds of thousands of people about their dining-out experiences.

Most of their reports are positive – proof of the ever-growing skill and dedication of the nation's chefs and restaurateurs. But inevitably, we also hear about problems.

Obviously, there are certain basics that everyone has the right to expect when dining out:

1) Courteous, hospitable, informative service

2) Clean, sanitary facilities

3) Fresh, healthful food

4) Timely honoring of reservations

5) Smoke-free seating

Sadly, if these conditions aren't met, many diners simply swallow their disappointment, assuming there's nothing they can do. However, the truth is that diners have far more power than they may realize.

Every restaurateur worth his or her salt wants to satisfy customers, since happy clients equal a successful business. Rather than the adversaries they sometimes seem to be, diners and restaurateurs are natural allies – both want the same outcome, and each can help the other achieve it.

Towards that end, here are a few simple but sometimes forgotten tips that every restaurant-goer should bear in mind:

1) Speak up: If dissatisfied by any aspect of your experience – from the handling of your reservation to the food, service or physical environment – tell the manager. Most problems are easy to resolve at the time they occur – but not if management doesn't know about them until afterward. The opposite is also true: if you're pleased, speak up.

2) Spell out your needs ahead of time: If you have specific dietary requests, wish to bring your own wine, want a smoke-free (or smoking) environment, or have any other special needs, you can avoid disappointment by calling ahead to make sure the restaurant can satisfy you.

3) Do your part: A restaurant's ability to honor reservations, for example, is largely dependent on diners honoring reservations and showing up on time. Make it a point to cancel reservations you're unable to use and be sure to notify the restaurant if you'll be late. The restaurant, in turn, should do its best to seat parties promptly, and, if there are delays, should keep diners informed (a free drink doesn't hurt either).

4) Vote with your dollars: Most people tip 15 to 19%, and often 20% or more at high-end restaurants. Obviously, you have the right not to tip at all if unhappy with the service; but in that case, many simply leave 10% to get the message across. If you like the restaurant, it's worth accompanying the low tip with a word to the management. Of course, the ultimate way to vote with your dollars is not to come back.

5) Put it in writing: Like it or not, all restaurants make mistakes. The best ones distinguish themselves by how well they acknowledge and handle mistakes. If you've expressed your complaints to the restaurant management but haven't gotten a satisfactory response, write to your local restaurant critic, with a copy to the restaurant, detailing the problem. That really gets the restaurateur's attention. Naturally, we also hope you'll express your feelings, pro and con, by voting on zagat.com.

Key to Ratings/Symbols

This sample entry identifies the various types of
information contained in your Zagat Survey.

(1) Restaurant Name, Address & Phone Number

(2) Hours & Credit Cards

(3) ZAGAT Surveyor Ratings

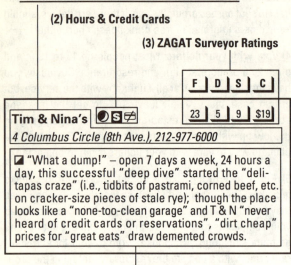

F	D	S	C
23	5	9	$19

Tim & Nina's ◐ 🅢 ⊄

4 Columbus Circle (8th Ave.), 212-977-6000

◪ "What a dump!" – open 7 days a week, 24 hours a
day, this successful "deep dive" started the "deli-
tapas craze" (i.e., tidbits of pastrami, corned beef, etc.
on cracker-size pieces of stale rye); though the place
looks like a "none-too-clean garage" and T & N "never
heard of credit cards or reservations", "dirt cheap"
prices for "great eats" draw demented crowds.

(4) Surveyors' Commentary

The names of restaurants with the highest overall ratings,
greatest popularity and importance are printed in **CAPITAL
LETTERS**. Address and phone numbers are printed in *italics*.

(2) Hours & Credit Cards

After each restaurant name you will find the following
courtesy information:

◐ .... *serving after 11 PM*

🅢 .... *open on Sunday*

⊄ .... *no credit cards accepted*

(3) ZAGAT Surveyor Ratings

Food, **Decor** and **Service** are each rated on a scale of **0** to **30**:

F	D	S	C

F	....	*Food*
D	....	*Decor*
S	....	*Service*
C	....	*Cost*

23	5	9	$19

0 - 9	....	*poor to fair*
10 - 15	....	*fair to good*
16 - 19	....	*good to very good*
20 - 25	....	*very good to excellent*
26 - 30	....	*extraordinary to perfection*

▽ 23	5	9	$19

▽ .... *Low number of votes/less reliable*

The **Cost (C)** column reflects surveyors' estimated price of a dinner with one drink and tip. Lunch usually costs 25% less.

A restaurant listed without ratings is either an important **newcomer** or a popular **write-in**. The estimated cost, with one drink and tip, is indicated by the following symbols.

–	–	–	VE

I	....	*$15 and below*
M	....	*$16 to $30*
E	....	*$31 to $50*
VE	....	*$51 or more*

(4) Surveyors' Commentary

Surveyors' comments are summarized, with literal comments shown in quotation marks. The following symbols indicate whether responses were mixed or uniform.

◪ .... *mixed*
◼ .... *uniform*

Most Popular Restaurants

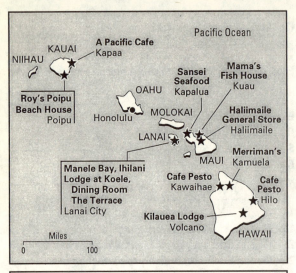

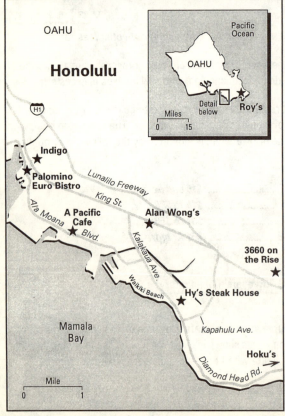

www.zagat.com

Most Popular Restaurants

Each of our reviewers has been asked to name his or her five favorite restaurants. The 20 spots most frequently named, in order of their popularity, are:

Big Island
1. Merriman's
2. Cafe Pesto
3. Kilauea Lodge

Kauai
1. Beach House
2. Roy's Poipu
3. A Pacific Cafe

Lanai
1. Lodge at Koele, Dining Room
2. Manele Bay, Ihilani
3. Lodge at Koele, The Terrace

Maui
1. Mama's Fish House
2. Haliimaile Gen. Store
3. Sansei Seafood

Oahu
1. Alan Wong's
2. Hoku's
3. Roy's
4. 3660 on the Rise
5. Indigo
6. Palomino Euro Bistro
7. A Pacific Cafe
8. Hy's Steak House

It's obvious that many of the restaurants on the above list are among the most expensive, but Hawaiian Islanders also love a bargain. Were popularity calibrated to price, we suspect that a number of other restaurants would join the above ranks. Thus, we have listed 25 Best Buys on page 18.

Top Ratings*

Top 20 Food Ranking

27 Alan Wong's
Lodge at Koele, Dining Rm./L
Roy's Poipu/K
La Bourgogne/H
26 Anuenue Room/M
A Pacific Cafe/K
La Mer
Waterfront/M
Roy's
Sansei Seafood/M

Merriman's/H
Hoku's
Roy's Nicolina/M
Ruth's Chris
Roy's Kahana/M
David Paul's Lahaina/M
A Saigon Cafe/M
Manele Bay, Ihilani/L
25 Yohei Sushi
Haliimaile Gen. Store/M

Top Spots by Cuisine

American (New)
27 Lodge at Koele, Dining Rm./L
26 David Paul's Lahaina Grill/M
25 Haliimaile Gen. Store/M
24 Seaside Rest./H
23 Henry Clay's/L

American (Traditional)
25 Hy's Steak House
23 Ono Family Rest./K
22 Kincaid's
Plantation House of Poipu/K
Manago Hotel Rest./H

Breakfast
23 Ono Family Rest./K
Manele Bay, Hulopo'e Ct./L
Eggs 'n Things
21 Aloha Cafe/H
20 Charley's/M

Brunch
25 Orchids
23 Prince Court Rest.
22 Plumeria Beach Cafe
Gaylord's/Kilohana/K
20 Hanohano Room

Buffet Dining
23 Prince Court Rest.
Manele Bay, Hulopo'e Ct./L
22 Parc Cafe
Plumeria Beach Cafe
20 Cafe Hanalei/K

Chinese
24 Golden Dragon
Legend Seafood
23 Royal Garden
22 Hong Kong Noodle
21 Kirin

Continental
26 Waterfront/M
24 Kilauea Lodge/H
Edelweiss Rest./H
Swiss Inn
Alfred's

Dim Sum
24 Legend Seafood
23 Royal Garden
20 Eastern Garden
Panda Cuisine
Hee Hing

Eclectic/International
26 Hoku's
23 Tai-Pan on Blvd.
Cafe Pesto/H
Maha's Cafe/H
22 Casa Di Amici/K

Eurasian
27 Roy's Poipu/K
26 Roy's
Roy's Nicolina/M
Roy's Kahana/M
25 Roy's Waikoloa/H

---

* Excluding restaurants with low voting. All restaurants are located
on the island of Oahu unless otherwise noted (H=Big Island of
Hawaii; K=Kauai; L=Lanai; M=Maui and MO=Molokai).

Top Food

French
27 La Bourgogne/H
26 La Mer
25 Chez Paul/M
24 Duc's Bistro
23 Michel's

Hamburgers
22 Duane's Ono-Char/K
Kua'Aina Sandwich
18 Bubba Burgers/K
16 Big City Diner - Kaimuki
Hard Rock Cafe

Hawaiian Regional
27 Alan Wong's
26 Anuenue Room/M
A Pacific Cafe/K
Merriman's/H
Roy's Kahana/M

Hotel Dining
27 Lodge at Koele, Dining Rm./L
26 Anuenue Room/M
La Mer
Hoku's
Manele Bay, Ihilani/L

Italian
25 Piatti/K
24 Dondero's/K
Donatoni's/H
Pomodoro/K
22 Nick's Fishmarket

Japanese (Local Style)
26 Sansei Seafood/M
24 L'Uraku
23 Yanagi Sushi
Tokyo Tei/M
21 Teshima/H

Japanese (Tokyo Style)
25 Yohei Sushi
Kyo-Ya
24 Restaurant Kintaro/K
Hakone/M
23 Restaurant Suntory

Local Food
23 Ono Hawaiian Foods
22 Hamura Saimin/K
Sam Choy's Kaloko/H
Manago Hotel Rest./H
21 Kakaako Kitchen

Mediterranean
26 Manele Bay, Ihilani/L
23 Plantation House/M
22 Azul
Palomino Euro Bistro
21 Edward's/Kanaloa/H

Mexican
20 Tres Hombres/H
El Burrito
18 Maui Tacos
16 Azteca
Compadres

Pacific Rim
27 Roy's Poipu/K
26 Roy's
25 3660 on the Rise
Swan Court/M
Roy's Waikoloa/H

Pizza
25 Brick Oven Pizza/K
23 Cafe Pesto/H
19 California Pizza Kitchen
18 Boston's North End Pizza
16 Harpo's

Seafood
26 Waterfront/M
Sansei Seafood/M
25 Orchids
Mama's Fish House/M
24 Nick's Fishmarket/M

Steakhouses
26 Ruth's Chris
25 Hy's Steak House
22 Kincaid's
21 Kalaheo Steak House/K
Kobe

Sushi
26 Sansei Seafood/M
25 Yohei Sushi
24 Hakone/H
23 Restaurant Suntory
Yanagi Sushi

Thai
25 Mekong Thai
23 Singha Thai
Keo's
22 Chiang Mai
21 Saeng's/M

Top Food

Vietnamese
26 A Saigon Cafe/M
24 Duc's Bistro
22 Hale Vietnam
19 Little Bit of Saigon
18 Ba-Le French

Yearlings
25 Padovani's
24 Nick's Fishmarket/M
   A Pacific Cafe/M
23 Chef Mavro's
21 Jacques Bistro/M

Top Spots by Island

Big Island
27 La Bourgogne
26 Merriman's
25 Roy's Waikoloa

Maui
26 Anuenue Room
   Waterfront
   Sansei Seafood

Kauai
27 Roy's Poipu
26 A Pacific Cafe
25 Beach House

Oahu
27 Alan Wong's
26 La Mer
   Roy's

Lanai
27 Lodge at Koele, Dining Rm.
26 Manele Bay, Ihilani
23 Henry Clay's

Top 20 Decor Ranking

29	Old Lahaina Luau/M		Swan Court/M
28	Lodge at Koele, Dining Rm./L		Nick's Fishmarket/M
	Brown's Beach Hse./H	25	Hau Tree Lanai
27	Orchids		Ilima Terrace/K
	La Mer		Bali-By-The-Sea
	Tidepools/K		Duke's Canoe Club/K
	Beach House/K		Michel's
26	Hoku's		Anuenue Room/M
	Canoe House/H		Palomino Euro Bistro
	Manele Bay, Ihilani/L		Dondero's/K

Open-Air Rooms

Bali-By-The-Sea
Brown's Beach Hse./H
Canoe House/H
Coast Grille/H
Hau Tree Lanai

Manele Bay, Hulopo'e Ct./L
Manele Bay, Ihilani/L
Orchids
Seasons/M
Tidepools/K

Romantic

Bay Club/M
Chef Mavro's
Dondero's/K
Kilauea Lodge/H
La Mer

Manele Bay, Ihilani/L
Pahu i'a/H
Seasons/M
Swan Court/M
Waterfront/M

Rooms

Anuenue Room/M
Azul
Golden Dragon
Hoku's

Nick's Fishmarket/M
Prince Court
Surf Room
Swan Court/M

Views

Beach House/K
Cafe Hanalei/K
Edward's/Kanaloa/H
Hanohano Room
Hula Grill/M
Kula Lodge/M

Leilani's on Beach/M
Mama's Fish House/M
Old Lahaina Luau/M
pacific'O/M
Seawatch/M
Shells/K

Top 20 Service Ranking

27	Anuenue Room/M	24	Dondero's/K
	Lodge at Koele, Dining Rm./L		Orchids
26	La Mer		Brown's Beach Hse./H
	Nick's Fishmarket/M		Swiss Inn
25	Old Lahaina Luau/M		Chez Paul/M
	Gerard's/M		Pomodoro/K
	Hoku's		Swan Court/M
	Waterfront/M		Hakone/M
	Manele Bay, Ihilani/L		Canoe House/H
	Alan Wong's		La Bourgogne/H

Best Buys

25 Top Bangs For The Buck

This list reflects the best dining values in our *Survey*. It is produced by dividing the cost of a meal into the combined ratings for food, decor and service.

1. Andy's Sandwiches
2. Hamura Saimin/K
3. Maui Tacos/H
4. Don's Grill/H
5. Bubba Burgers/K
6. Ba-Le French
7. Kua'Aina Sandwich
8. Hong Kong Noodle
9. Duane's Ono-Char/K
10. Eggs 'n Things
11. Coffee Gallery
12. Sam Sato's/M
13. Island Manapua Factory
14. Kalaheo Coffee Co./K
15. Grace's Drive Inn
16. Cafe Laufer
17. Mocha Java
18. Kanemitsu Bakery/MO
19. Boston's North End Pizza
20. Ono Family Rest./K
21. Maui Tacos
22. Jimbo
23. Manago Hotel Rest./H
24. Joe's Courtside Cafe/K
25. El Burrito

Alphabetical
Directory of
Restaurants

Big Island of Hawaii

TOP 3 FOOD RANKING

	Restaurant	Cuisine Type
27	La Bourgogne	Classic French
26	Merriman's	Hawaiian Regional
25	Roy's Waikoloa	Pacific Rim

F	D	S	C

Aloha Cafe 🅢 — 21 | 17 | 18 | $15
Aloha Theater Complex, Hwy. 11, Kainaliu, 808-322-3383
■ The "cheery staff" gives real "aloha" at this "charming" little cafe which wraps around a historic theater 1,500 feet above Kainaliu; to complement the partial ocean view and local artwork, there's "good, healthy" Eclectic fare highlighted by "great breakfasts", "huge" sandwiches, lots of vegetarian options and "yummy" homemade desserts.

Bamboo Restaurant 🅢 — 22 | 22 | 19 | $27
Hwy. 270/Akoni Pule Hwy. (Hwy. 250), Hawi, 808-889-5555
☑ For a "slice of the '40s in Hawaii", consider this "quaint" "tropical paradise" set in a plantation-era building in Hawi; it's a "must stop" for "creative", "affordable" Hawaiian Regional cuisine and "spontaneous hula" dancing.

Batik, The 🅢 — ▽ 23 | 23 | 22 | $54
Mauna Kea Beach Hotel, 62-100 Mauna Kea Beach Dr., Kamuela, 808-882-5801
■ Located just outside of Kawaihae, this "lovely", dinner-only room in the Big Island's oldest resort hotel allows "special-event" patrons to kick back in Far Eastern–themed, "old-style" luxury as they dine on impeccably served Eurasian victuals; N.B. closed during the summer months.

Bay Terrace, The 🅢 — ▽ 19 | 21 | 19 | $34
Mauna Lani Bay Hotel & Bungalows, 68-1400 Mauna Lani Dr., Kohala Coast, 808-885-6622
■ This Kohala resort seafooder is primarily known for its "wonderful" breakfast buffet but is also open for dinner in season; atmospheric diversions along the lines of watching the sun set over the top of Mauna Kea or taking in the surrounding palm trees add to the overall lush ambiance.

Bianelli's Pizza 🅢 — 21 | 13 | 17 | $16
75-240 Nani Kailua Dr., Kailua-Kona, 808-326-4800
☑ "Tasty", "gourmet" deep-dish and thin-crust pizzas, which just might be "the best on Big Island", draw "groups" and "families" to this "neighborhood joint" at the Pines Plaza in Kailua; still, naysayers sigh this "overrated" spot is "steadily going downhill."

Big Island Steak House ◐🅂   17 18 17 $25
*Kings' Shops, 250 Waikoloa Beach Dr., Waikoloa,
808-886-8805*
■ A "convenient Waikoloa location" in a Kohala Coast
mini-mall draws locals and tourists alike to this "tasty" chop
shop with some of the "best ribs since Adam"; though
service can sometimes be "damn slow", it is "great for
kids", not to mention late-nighters, as the kitchen closes
at 11:30 PM.

BROWN'S BEACH HOUSE 🅂   24 28 24 $40
*Orchid at Mauna Lani, 1 N. Kaniku Dr., Kohala Coast,
808-885-2000*
■ "Beautiful alfresco dining" in a "spectacular" beachfront
setting, "attentive service", hula dancing and "great"
Hawaiian Regional cuisine add up to high scores for this
Kohala Coast achiever; just remember to "bring a wrap"
("because the wind can pick up") and save room for the
"wonderful" caramel insanity cake; N.B. chef David Reardon
recently departed, putting the above food rating in question.

Cafe Pesto 🅂   23 18 20 $22
*308 Kamehameha Ave. (Mamo St.), Hilo, 808-969-6640
Kawaihae Shopping Ctr., Hwy. 270, Kawaihae, 808-882-1071*
☑ Located on opposite sides of the island in Hilo and
Kawaihae, these Eclectic siblings win raves for their
"excellent" light entrees, pizzas, calzones, salads and
pastas; moreover, the "casual", "cafe-style" settings allow
enough room so "you're not sitting in someone's lap."

Canoe House 🅂   24 26 24 $51
*Mauna Lani Bay Hotel & Bungalows, 68-1400 Mauna Lani Dr.,
Kohala Coast, 808-885-6622*
■ An "elegant", "romantic" location "next to the ocean"
is the backdrop for this "classy" Pacific Rim eatery in
Kohala where "excellent" dishes such as nori-wrapped
tempura ahi are just the thing for those "pricey", "special-
occasion" dinners; nonetheless, diehards say it's "hard to
forget" what the cooking was like under former chef Alan
Wong (even though it's been five years since he left).

Chart House   19 19 18 $29
Waterfront Row, 75-5770 Alii Dr., Kailua-Kona, 808-329-2451
See review in Oahu Directory.

Coast Grille 🅂   ▽ 23 24 19 $48
*Hapuna Beach Prince Hotel, 62-100 Kauna'oa Dr.
(Queen Kaahumanu Hwy.), Kohala Coast, 808-880-1111*
■ "Creative" Hawaiian Regional cuisine and a "winning"
raw bar ("terrific clams") complement a sunset view of
the Pacific at this dinner-only resort dining room on a bluff
above Hapuna Beach; reservations are recommended,
especially for the coveted terrace tables.

Donatoni's S   24 | 24 | 24 | $42
*Hilton Waikoloa Village, 425 Waikoloa Beach Dr.
(Queen Kaahamanu Hwy.), Waikoloa, 808-886-1234*
■ Situated along a canal in the Hilton Waikoloa Village,
this tribute to the red, white and green features Venetian-
themed "old-world" decor, first-rate service and chef Sascia
Marchese's light touch with "yummy" Northern Italian
food, which some think rivals the "best on the island."

Don's Grill S   22 | 16 | 23 | $11
485 Hinano St. (Kekuanaoa St.), Hilo, 808-935-9099
■ "Zippy service" and "cheap" prices are the hallmarks of
this Hilo Hawaiian, which serves "consistently good"
"comfort food" in a "charming island" setting; it's "casual
enough for the kids" or "for grandma after church."

Edelweiss Restaurant   24 | 19 | 22 | $30
Kawaihae Rd., Waimea, 808-885-6800
■ "Huge" portions of "delicious" Continental victuals come
courtesy of chef Hans Peter at this "quaint" "old-world"
spot in the rolling hills of Waimea where regulars "don't
order from the menu" but rather opt for the "incredible
specials"; even naysayers who find the food "too salty"
and "heavy" readily concede that "the staff is a blast"
and that prices are "fair."

Edward's at Kanaloa S   21 | 23 | 20 | $35
Kanaloa at Kona, 78-261 Manukai St., Kailua-Kona, 808-322-1434
■ Lotharios seeking a "great romantic spot" should
consider this "beautiful" water's edge Mediterranean in
south Kona that many call a "wonderful surprise"; its
"unique menu" includes such signature dishes as peppered
ahi, Aegean salmon and flourless chocolate cake.

Fiascos S   16 | 15 | 18 | $17
200 Kanoelehua Ave., Hilo, 808-935-7666
☑ Despite its unpromising name, this "cheap" Eclectic
outside of Downtown Hilo features a "great salad bar" as
well as a wide variety of "straightforward" vittles; fans
say it's a "good place to meet for business or pleasure",
though foes deride the "tired decor" and "slow service."

Hakone S   ▽ 23 | 21 | 19 | $41
*Hapuna Beach Prince Hotel, 62-100 Kauna'oa Dr.
(Queen Kaahumanu Hwy.), Kohala Coast, 808-880-1111*
■ The "excellent dinner buffet" and "best sushi bar" are
the stars at this prestigious Kohala Coast hotel dining room
where the Japanese authenticity extends to the setting,
which was fashioned from materials imported from the Land
of the Rising Sun; N.B. open Saturday–Wednesday only.

Hard Rock Cafe S   16 | 21 | 16 | $19
*Coconut Grove Mktpl., 75-5815 Alii Dr. (off of Kuakini),
Kailua-Kona, 808-329-8866*
See review in Oahu Directory.

Harrington's S   20 | 20 | 20 | $29 |
135 Kalanianaole Hwy. (Ice Pond at Reed's Bay), Hilo,
808-961-4966
☑ A "beautiful waterside setting" overlooking Reed's Bay
whets appetites for the "very good" American fare ("go for
the prime rib and fish") at this Hilo staple; yet even "attentive"
service that's "never pretentious" can't stop cutting-edge
culinarians from carping that the menu is "outdated."

Hualalai Club Grille S   23 | 25 | 23 | $33 |
Four Seasons Resort Hualalai, 100 Kaupulehu Dr.,
Kaupulehu-Kona, 808-325-8525
■ "After a tough day on the links", this "fabulous" (if
"pricey") open-air spot overlooking both the ocean and
the 18th hole of the Hualalai Golf Course offers "creative"
Pacific Rim fare, an "excellent" California-focused wine
list and "outstanding service"; though peace lovers find it
"very serene", livelier types fret it's "almost too quiet."

Huggo's S   20 | 22 | 19 | $31 |
75-5828 Kahakai Rd. (Alii Dr.), Kailua-Kona, 808-329-1493
☑ To observe a "smashing" sunset view (and maybe even
the famous green flash), head to this "reliable" Hawaiian
Regional on the ocean in Kailua-Kona; twentysomethings
add that dancing and entertainment in the open-air Huggo's
On the Rocks (next door) ensure an "active bar scene."

Jameson's by the Sea S   18 | 19 | 18 | $29 |
Kona Magic Sands, 75-6452 Alii Dr., Kailua-Kona, 808-329-3195
See review in Oahu Directory.

Kamuela Provision Company   22 | 22 | 21 | $34 |
Hilton Waikoloa Village, 425 Waikoloa Beach Dr.
(Queen Kaahamanu Hwy.), Waikoloa, 808-886-1234
■ Perched at the ocean's edge, this "down-home" Pacific
Rimmer in a Kohala resort boasts "romantic" sunset views to
complement its seafood and steaks; the "tropical trading
post" decor and live entertainment (Thursday–Saturday)
contribute to the "paradise perfect" feel.

Kawaihae Harbor Grill S   22 | 18 | 19 | $30 |
Kawaihae Ctr., Kawaihae, 808-882-1368
☑ Those in search of a "casual, local" island experience
turn to this Kawaihae seafood specialist; the downscale
digs are "very authentic", the "chef loves to cook" and the
service is "warm" and personal – "not a bad meal" at all.

Keei Cafe ⊘   ▽ 28 | 15 | 22 | $23 |
83-4587 Mamalahoa Hwy., Captain Cook, 808-328-8451
■ For native island dishes in a hole-in-the-wall setting,
this "funky" former fish market south of Captain Cook
delivers a "delicious menu" in "humongous" portions;
with its "great" service and "very reasonable" prices, it's
"gotten so popular, you need reservations."

Ken's House of Pancakes ◗ S   16   11   18 $12
1730 Kamehameha Ave., Hilo, 808-538-1877

☑ Hilo's only 24-hour coffee shop serves up "reliable" "local food" and "classic" breakfasts ("excellent pancakes"); it's known for "generous portions", "cheap" tabs, "sweet waitresses" and an ultracasual look, and is handy for jet setters as it's near the airport.

Kilauea Lodge & Restaurant S   24   25   23 $35
19-4055 Old Volcano Rd. (Wright Rd.), Volcano, 808-967-7366

☑ Up 4,000 feet in the tiny village of Volcano, this "mountain lodge" offers "comfy" fireside dining for "chilly evenings" and "superb" Continental cuisine (including the signature duck à l'orange) courtesy of a "creative, adventurous chef"; with ambiance that's "like someone's home", it's "not far from town in miles, but a world apart."

Koa House Grill S   18   18   18 $29
65-1144 Mamalahoa Hwy. (Hwy. 19), Kamuela, 808-885-2088

☑ A "nice addition" to the growing number of outposts in the mountain town of Waimea, this New American wins favor for its "excellent ahi", Angus beef and "sophisticated cowboy" trappings; a few foes rule it "limited" and warn "vegetarians need not apply."

Kona Inn Restaurant S   19   23   20 $28
Kona Inn Village Shopping Ctr., 75-5744 Alii Dr., Kailua-Kona, 808-329-4455

■ Exuding a "magnificent feeling of old Hawaii", this "relaxing", open-air New American sits "right by the water" in Kailua-Kona; with its "surprisingly good, creative" cooking, it's the perfect place to meet "on the beach for sunset" or for a "romantic" rendezvous.

Kona Ranch House S   18   16   18 $18
75-5653 Ololi St. (Hwy. 11, bet. Kuakini & Palani Sts.), Kailua-Kona, 808-329-7061

■ This Traditional American in the heart of Kailua-Kona is "always dependable" for "family eats", including a "great breakfast" with homemade cornbread; regulars dub it "the Denny's of Kona" for its "coffee shop" setting and "laid-back" approach; N.B. breakfast and lunch only.

Kona Village Luau   ▽ 25   25   23   VE
Kona Village Resort, Queen Kaahumanu Hwy., Kailua-Kona, 808-325-5555

☑ Every Friday night in an oasis in Kaupulehu on the slopes of Hualalai, "the best luau on the island" gets underway at this easygoing resort, complete with "outstanding", authentic Hawaiian dishes and Polynesian entertainment; formerly for hotel guests only, the *hale* (thatched hut) is now open to all.

LA BOURGOGNE   27   21   24 $42
Kuakini Plaza S., 77-6400 Nalani St. (Hwy. 11),
Kailua-Kona, 808-329-6711
■ Located halfway between Kailua-Kona and Keauhou, this
"very small", "very French" "hidden treasure" features
"delicious" Classic Gallic fare matched with "personal"
service and an "intimate" ambiance; the tone is "formal" –
maybe even "slightly arrogant" – but "everything is great,
even the desserts"; N.B. dinner only, reservations required.

Maha's Cafe S   23   20   21 $18
Waimea Shopping Ctr., 65-1148 Mamalahoa Hwy.,
Waimea, 808-885-0693
■ Chef-owner Maha Kraan showcases her "tasty",
"healthy" Eclectic recipes (e.g. the signature smoked ahi)
and impeccable sense of style (everything is served on
antique china) at this "quaint" and "comfortable" "tea
room"; the "unique setting" is a 19th-century missionary
home in the cool Upcountry of Waimea; N.B. breakfast
and lunch only.

Manago Hotel Restaurant S   22   13   21 $14
Manago Hotel, 622-6155 Mamalohoa Hwy., Captain Cook,
808-323-2642
☑ "'40s-style" "old Hawaii dining" is alive and well at this
"landmark" in a "funky but chic" historic hotel in Captain
Cook; the "solid" American-Hawaiian fare ("best pork chops
around") is still served "family-style" at "long tables" – a
rare revival of Kona's bygone "coffee culture."

Maui Tacos S   18   11   14 $11
Prince Kuhio Plaza, 111 E. Puainakoo Hwy. (Kanoelehua Ave.),
Hilo, 808-959-0359
See review in Maui Directory.

MERRIMAN'S RESTAURANT S   26   22   24 $38
Opelo Plaza, Hwy. 19 (Opelo Rd.), Kamuela, 808-885-6822
■ Once again this "constantly superb" Waimea Hawaiian
Regional has been voted the Big Island's Most Popular
eatery, largely due to chef-owner Peter Merriman's
"innovative, fresh and delicious" cuisine (e.g. wok-charred
ahi, corn-and-shrimp fritters); citing the "charming"
atmosphere and "concerned" staff, its merry fans declare
they "can't get there often enough."

Ninon Restaurant   22   19   20 $21
123 Lihiwai St. (Banyan Dr.), Hilo, 808-969-1133
■ With a "great location" overlooking Hilo Bay on one
side and the Liliuokalani Gardens on the other, this
"authentic" Japanese provides a "calming setting"
(probably because it's "a bit isolated"); its selection of the
"freshest" sushi and sashimi around further elates fans.

Ocean View Inn 🅂⊘ | 17 | 11 | 14 | $15 |
75-5683 Alii Drive (Kuakini Rd.), Kailua-Kona, 808-329-1443
■ "What a view!"; overlooking Kailua Bay, this "real local place" with "really cheap" prices specializes in "home-cooked" Hawaiian fare in a "funky to da max" space; "slow" service irks clock-watchers, though otherwise they pronounce it "classic in every way."

Oodles of Noodles 🅂 | 23 | 19 | 18 | $20 |
Cross Roads, 75-1027 Henry St. (Mamalahoa Hwy.), Kailua-Kona, 808-329-9222
🅉 Chef Amy Ferguson Ota sure "knows her noodles" at this "casual and yummy" Kona Eclectic where the "innovative", "mouthwatering" options range from pad Thai to pasta; though the outdoor tables have a "parking lot view", there is indoor seating and "great takeout" also available.

Orchid Court 🅂 | ▽ 22 | 22 | 20 | $32 |
Orchid at Mauna Lani, 1 N. Kaniku Dr., Kohala Coast, 808-885-2000
🅉 In a "lovely setting" on the garden level of a Kohala Coast resort with ocean views, this hotel Californian offers a "great breakfast buffet" in the morning and "well-prepared" dinners come sunset; faithful fans have only one lament: "wish we could go more often"; N.B. reservations required.

Pahu i'a 🅂 | ▽ 27 | 29 | 27 | $56 |
Four Seasons Resort Hualalai, 100 Kaupulehu Dr., Kaupulehu-Kona, 808-325-8333
■ With its "sublime" beachfront locale at Hualalai, this "too romantic" New American–International might be the "most beautiful restaurant on the Big Island" – and that's just the beginning; surveyors sigh this is "perfect" "grand dining", from the "outstanding" specialties (e.g. tempura-style shrimp and asparagus brochettes) to the "great wine list" to the "best service" money can buy.

Palm Cafe 🅂 | – | – | – | E |
Coconut Grove Market, 75-5805 Alii Dr., Kailua-Kona, 808-329-8200
Closed for over a year, this Hawaiian Regional is back in business at a new location in the Coconut Grove Marketplace, just a few doors down from its former locale; now under the helm of chef Kevin Nutt (ex Cafe Pesto), it features the same casual, open-air atmosphere, but now boasts a better view of the rolling surf of Kailua Bay.

Paniolo Country Inn 🅂 | 18 | 15 | 18 | $16 |
65-1214 Lindsey Rd. (Hwy. 19), Kamuela, 808-885-4377
🅉 "Good plain fare" and "excellent value" bring buckaroos to this "family-type" Waimea American for "huge portions" of "country-style" cooking – think "stews and steaks" – served in a convincing "cowboy" milieu; a "filling" and "friendly" time is had by all.

Parker Ranch Grill ⑤   20 | 22 | 18 | $27
Parker Ranch Ctr., 67-1185A Mamalahoa Hwy. (Lindsey Rd.),
Kamuela, 808-887-2624
◪ Hankering for a "great steak"?; this Waimea "Wild West"
outpost is a "comfortable" "neighborhood" meatery with
a "cozy" fireplace and plenty of *paniolo* (island cowpoke)
credibility; other pluses include a "friendly" staff and hefty
burgers that only "a big mouth" can handle.

Pescatore ⑤   21 | 18 | 21 | $25
235 Keawe St. (Haili St.), Hilo, 808-969-9090
◪ Mama mia – "a real Italian restaurant in Hilo!"; this
"dark", "intimate" Downtowner specializes in seafood
(carpaccio with ahi, cioppino) with "lots of bold flavors"
and combined with "impeccable service", locals are
learning to "love it, love it, love it."

Quinn's Almost-By-The-Sea ●⑤ ▽   22 | 14 | 17 | $19
75-5655 Palani Rd., Kailua-Kona, 808-329-3822
◼ One of the few Kailua-Kona entries to keep late hours, this
"fun little place" offers a light Continental menu rounded out
by faves like the "Quinnburger" and "great fish and chips";
the patio out back makes it a winner "for lunch" too.

Reuben's Mexican Restaurant   17 | 11 | 13 | $16
336 Kamehameha Ave. (Mamo St.), Hilo, 808-961-6100
◪ Featuring some of the "best margaritas" and "hottest
salsa" around, this "popular" Hilo spot has a "small town
in Mexico" feel, complete with "slow service" and iffy digs;
amigos insist it's "worth dealing with" for the "cheap" eats.

Roussels ⑤   20 | 16 | 18 | $27
Waikoloa Village Golf Club, 68-1792 Melia St., Waikoloa
Village, 808-883-9644
◪ "Conveniently" perched above the Waikoloa Village
links, this "wonderful" Cajun-Creole specialist brings
"tasty" down-home dishes like Louisiana crawfish and
gumbo to the tropics; with its "relaxed atmosphere", it
encourages that Big Easy insouciance.

Royal Siam   24 | 13 | 18 | $18
70 Mamo St. (Keawe St.), Hilo, 808-961-6100
◼ Some of the Big Island's best Thai cooking awaits at this
"quaint" Downtown Hilo Siamese, hailed for its "excellent,
authentic" tastes and consistent "value"; aficionados are
happy to be "hooked" on the royal treatment.

Roy's Waikoloa Bar & Grill ⑤   25 | 20 | 21 | $38
Kings' Shops, 250 Waikoloa Beach Dr. (Waikoloa Beach Resort),
Waikoloa, 808-886-4321
◪ Impresario Roy Yamaguchi's "gorgeous" Waikoloa Pacific
Rimmer serves as a showcase for chef Jacqueline Lau's
"creative cuisine" ("don't miss the chocolate soufflé")
delivered by a "friendly staff"; the "energetic" atmosphere is
"typical Roy's", meaning "noisy" but "pleasant."

Sam Choy's Kaloko S   22 | 11 | 18 | $21
73-5576 Kauhola Bay (Kaloko Industrial Park),
Kailua-Kona, 808-326-1545
■ "Zero ambiance but great food" says it all; secluded in a warehouse outside Kailua-Kona, this "unique" "family place" is famed for its "huge portions" of "basic" Pacific Rim and "local-style" delicacies ("great fried poke"); still a "must-stop for visitors", this is the "Sam's original" that spawned the semi-ubiquitous chain.

Seaside Restaurant S   24 | 15 | 20 | $21
1790 Kalanianaole Ave. (Lokoaka St.), Hilo, 808-935-8825
■ "Fresh fish" takes on new meaning at this "fabulous" local-style New American, which boasts a "unique setting" overlooking ponds stocked with the mullet, trout, catfish, golden perch and *aholehole* (Hawaiian flagtail) that wind up on your plate; it's located just beyond Radio Bay in Hilo, so "call ahead" for a good table and get the "full value."

Sibu Cafe S⊄   23 | 13 | 18 | $18
Banyan Court Mall, 75-5695 Alii Dr. (bet. the Palace & the Pier),
Kailua-Kona, 808-329-1112
■ Hidden in a row of shops along Alii Drive in Kailua-Kona, this "excellent, low-key" Indonesian offers ultra-"casual" dining; those in search of a "filling meal" and "good dollar value" find it "worth looking for."

Surt's at Volcano Village S   ∇ 23 | 17 | 22 | $28
Old Volcano Rd. (Humnani Rd.), Volcano Village, 808-967-8511
■ "What a surprise!"; it's "worth driving from Hilo just to eat" at this "remote" Asian-French fusion house where the "best food in Volcano" Village ("great curries") flows from chef Surt Thamountha's kitchen; with its "mellow atmosphere", this is true "country dining" and a true "find."

Teshima Restaurant S⊄   21 | 13 | 19 | $15
Mamalahoa Hwy. (bet. Buddhist Temple & Texaco),
Honalo, 808-322-9140
☑ Perched cliffside in Honalo, this Japanese-American is a "classic" local "institution"; a longtime supplier of "wonderful" noodles and tempura at a "reasonable cost", it complements its "comfort food" with a "homey", "family" approach and "'50s decor."

Tres Hombres Beach Grill S   20 | 18 | 16 | $20
Kawaihae Shopping Ctr. (Kawaihae Harbor), Kawaihae,
808-882-1031
Tres Hombres Steak & Seafood S
75-5864 Walua Rd. (Alii Dr.), Kailua-Kona, 808-329-2173
☑ "Mexican with an island flair" is the formula at this indoor/outdoor twosome in Kawaihae and Kailua-Kona; though south-of-the-border purists sniff at the "gringo" recipes, the "large portions" and "good variety" are convincing enough for its many compadres.

Kauai

F	D	S	C

A PACIFIC CAFE ⑤ | 26 | 20 | 23 | $40 |

Kauai Village Shopping Ctr., 4-831 Kuhio Hwy., Kapaa, 808-822-0013

■ Partisans proclaim this Kapaa "original" of chef Jean-Marie Josselin's "excellent" Hawaiian Regionals his "finest" effort; it's a "consistent winner" owing to its "outstanding food and wine list", and if a few find the "shopping center location" "odd", the "wonderful", "imaginative" fare and "awesome service" ensure it's still "hard to get a seat."

BEACH HOUSE RESTAURANT ⑤ | 25 | 27 | 22 | $41 |

5022 Lawai Rd. (off Poipu toward Spouting Horn), Lawai, 808-742-1424

☑ A "spectacular" oceanfront setting at Poipu ("sunsets to die for") coupled with "excellent", "creative eats" (wok-charred ahi, tiger-eye sushi) from a menu devised by chef Jean-Marie Josselin make this Hawaiian "joy" Kauai's Most Popular dining destination; N.B. chef Josselin is no longer in the kitchen, putting the above food rating into question.

Brennecke's Beach Broiler ⑤ | 19 | 20 | 18 | $25 |

2100 Hoone Rd. (opp. Poipu Beach Park), Poipu, 808-742-7588

☑ "Ocean breezes" and "nice views" provide the ambiance, and this open-air Poipu Beacher is perpetually crowded with the eternally tanned munching on burgers, seafood and pizza; despite grumbles that it's "all location", it remains the place for all the young dudes to "surf and sip."

Brick Oven Pizza ⑤ | 25 | 15 | 21 | $16 |

2-2555 Kaumualii Hwy., Kalaheo, 808-332-8561

■ "Best pizza on Kauai", "in Hawaii", "on the planet – period" exclaim pie pundits wowed by this "casual" pizzeria on the main highway in Kalaheo; special kudos go to the "delicious crust" as well as the staff's "good aloha spirit."

Bubba Burgers ⑤ | 18 | 14 | 16 | $10 |

5-5161 Kuhio Hwy., Hanalei, 808-826-7837

☑ There are usually "not enough seats" at this Hanalei burger "shack" that owes its popularity to "tasty" eats, "cool employees" and a "kick-in-the-pants" atmosphere; still, a few critics "like the T-shirts better than the food."

Bull Shed ⑤ | 21 | 17 | 19 | $26 |
796 Kuhio Hwy., Waipouli, Kapaa, 808-822-3791
☑ "Always crowded" yet "peaceful", Kapaa's "dependable" steakhouse-seafooder serves some of the "best rack of lamb" and prime rib around plus "excellent" oceanic fare, all enhanced by "good value" and a "beautiful view of crashing waves" outside; yet no reserving (for groups under 6) is admittedly "a bummer" and a few feel that after 27 years, this shed is "not what it used to be."

Cafe Hanalei ⑤ | 20 | 21 | 20 | $29 |
Princeville Hotel, 5520 Ka Haku Rd., Princeville, 808-826-2760
■ "Talk about romantic": "possibly the most spectacular view in Hawaii" – cloud-shrouded peaks rising above the sapphire water of Hanalei Bay – can be seen through the windows at this hotel dining room in Princeville; the Pacific Rim fare also earns praise, especially the "fabulous Sunday brunch" and "wonderful" Friday night seafood buffet.

Cafe Portofino ⑤ | 19 | 18 | 17 | $30 |
Pacific Ocean Plaza, 3501 Rice St. (opp. Marriott Hotel), Nawiliwili, 808-245-2121
☑ Though "not in a good location" (tucked inside a small shopping center just outside Lihue), this Mediterranean-Italian pleases most with its "authentic" fare (osso buco and rack of lamb are specialties), "great staff" and live harp music most nights; however, the less impressed claim the food goes "up and down in quality."

Caffe Coco ⑤   ▽ | 23 | 18 | 19 | $19 |
4-369 Kuhio Hwy., Kapaa, 808-822-7990
☑ "Delightfully different dining" in a tropical garden setting with "funky atmosphere" awaits at this "excellent" Eclectic–Pacific Rim restaurant set in a 1930s plantation house in Kapaa; it's open for breakfast, lunch and dinner, plus Sunday brunch, with live jazz nightly; N.B. closed Mondays.

Camp House Grill ⑤ | 18 | 12 | 19 | $14 |
King Kaumualii Hwy. (Papalina Rd.), Kalaheo, 808-332-9755
■ When hankering for "good, greasy", "basic American food", this "family" Kalaheo coffee shop can be "nirvana"; regulars ignore the "poor" decor and focus instead on the chicken, "awesome pies" and "excellent" breakfasts, all served in "huge portions" at "reasonable" prices.

Casa Di Amici ⑤ | 22 | 18 | 20 | $34 |
2301 Nalo Rd., Poipu, 808-742-1555
☑ "A real find" is what surveyors call this former North Shore eatery now relocated to Poipu: the "good" though "pricey" Eclectic-International food and "romantic" atmosphere (with a garden and outdoor patio) make it "a place to linger"; unfortunately, so does "slow service", according to a few critics; N.B. dinner only.

Kauai

F | D | S | C

Dondero's ⑤   24 | 25 | 24 | $46
Hyatt Regency Kauai, 1571 Poipu Rd., Poipu, 808-742-1234
☑ "Awesome", "the top rank of Italian food" gush admirers
of this "elegant" restaurant nestled in a romantic setting
at a top Poipu resort; whether dining on the patio or under
the Franciscan murals inside, it's "always a pleasure", with
the "best" staff and "good" wine selections; a few label it
"overpriced" and "pretentious", but they're outvoted.

Duane's Ono-Char Burger ⑤   22 | 11 | 15 | $10
4-4350 Kuhio Hwy., Anahola, 808-822-9181
☑ Trek into the jungle of Anahola, search out a roadside
hamburger stand that's really "just a take-out window"
and, our reviewers swear, you'll be rewarded with a "truly
awesome", "thick and juicy burger", "real potato fries" and
"killer" fruit shakes; but be prepared for stray chickens
waiting for handouts under the outdoor picnic tables.

Duke's Canoe Club ⑤   18 | 23 | 18 | $24
Kauai Marriott, Kalapaki Bay (Rice St.), Lihue, 808-246-9599
See review in Oahu Directory.

Eggbert's, The ⑤   19 | 14 | 17 | $14
Coconut Mktpl., 4-484 Kuhio Hwy., Kapaa, 808-822-3787
☑ Although this Eclectic eatery in Kapaa is open for lunch
and dinner, it's the all-day, "can't-be-beat" breakfasts that
bring in packs of "locals and tourists"; while some still
"miss the old location", the patio here has "nice views" of
Sleeping Giant Mountain.

Gaylord's At Kilohana ⑤   22 | 24 | 21 | $33
*Kilohana Estate, 3-2087 Kaumualii Hwy. (bet. Kauai
Community College & Kukui Grove), Lihue, 808-245-9593*
☑ Situated in a beautiful sprawling home on a 35-acre "old
plantation" just outside of Lihue, this Continental–Pacific Rim
venue is known for its "incredible ambiance", probably best
appreciated from the lanai looking up at Kilohana crater;
while it's "fine for special occasions", some call the
experience "overrated" owing to "not much competition."

Green Garden ⑤   17 | 14 | 18 | $17
Hwy. 50, Hanapepe, 808-335-5422
☑ This plant-filled eatery in the old plantation community of
Hanapepe serves a "wide variety" of "reasonably" priced
Eclectic fare including a "wonderful *lilikoi* pie"; therefore,
it's not surprising that it's "tour bus heaven" at lunch and
popular with families at dinner.

Hamura Saimin Stand ●⑤✏   22 | 10 | 16 | $9
2956 Kress St., Lihue, 808-245-3271
■ The hands-down "best *saimin* on Kauai" is served at this
"fun" Asian stand in Lihue, a local "landmark" where it helps
to ignore the "time warp" decor, "hard stools" and lack of AC
and concentrate instead on the "wonderful" "cheap eats";
N.B. it's one of the few eateries on the island open late.

Hanalei Dolphin Restaurant & Fish Market ⑤
20 | 20 | 16 | $27

5-5016 Kuhio Hwy., Hanalei, 808-826-6113

◩ "Great" "fresh fish" and a "beautiful river view" are the attractions at this dark wood–filled seafooder-steakhouse in Hanalei, which also has its own market for those who wish to grill their ahi, mahi mahi and swordfish at home.

Hanalei Wake-Up Cafe ⑤⊘
∇ 16 | 15 | 13 | $11

5-5144 Kuhio Hwy., Hanalei, 808-826-5551

◩ Despite middling ratings, some insist this "tiny" "surfer dude place" in Hanalei is the "best spot for an early breakfast" on the North Shore; expect a morning menu of American grub along with "old-fashioned island fare" served in an interior filled with "cool" historic photos of the town and its citizens.

Hanamaulu Restaurant ⑤
20 | 19 | 20 | $19

3-4291 Kuhio Hwy., Hanamaulu, 808-245-2511

■ This "Kauai legend" (since 1925) offers Chinese-Japanese fare and a choice of three seating options: a "serene" tea garden with koi pond, a sushi bar or American-style tables; takeout is available for the same "reasonable" prices, but then you'd miss out on the "beautiful" surroundings and "friendly" staff.

Hanapepe Cafe & Express Bar
22 | 18 | 23 | $23

3830 Hanapepe Rd. (Hwy. 50), Hanapepe, 808-335-5011

■ "A hidden gem", this "quaint", art-filled 'gourmet Vegetarian' (with an Italian flair) is "worth the drive" to Hanapepe for its "old soda bar", "wonderful" homemade breads and live Hawaiian slack key guitar; breakfast and lunch, Tuesday–Saturday, dinner Friday–Saturday only.

House of Seafood ⑤
21 | 19 | 20 | $38

1941 Poipu Rd., Poipu, 808-742-6433

◩ One of the "largest selections of local fish" on the island is available at this "excellent", plant-filled Poipu seafooder that also features such diverse items as flaming desserts and Caesar salad made tableside; "friendly" service somewhat appeases budget-watchers who mutter about "pricey" tabs.

Ilima Terrace ⑤
22 | 25 | 22 | $30

Hyatt Regency Kauai, 1571 Poipu Rd., Poipu, 808-742-1234

◩ The "beautiful setting" overlooking a tropical garden and lagoon stocked with brilliantly colored fish sets the "lovely" tone at this New American perched in a luxurious Poipu hotel; it also earns kudos for its Sunday champagne brunch buffet ("the best on Kauai") and a staff that's so "relaxed" "they didn't scold my wife for feeding the birds."

JJ's Broiler ⑤   18 | 20 | 17 | $23

Anchor Cove Shopping Ctr., 3416 Rice St., Lihue,
808-246-4422

☑ Locals drop by this sailing-themed New American seafooder just outside of Lihue for its "beautiful" waterfront view of Kalapaki Bay and winning Slavonic steak ("the bomb"); however, even the tasty mahi mahi sandwich can't convince wet blankets that the cooking is anything more than "ok."

Joe's Courtside Cafe ⑤   20 | 19 | 20 | $15

Kiahuna Tennis Club, 2290 Poipu Rd., Poipu, 808-742-6363

☑ "Great breakfasts" and lunches and a pleasant open-air patio overlooking the Kiahuna Tennis Club garner "solid" scores for this "casual" Cal-American in Poipu; "good guy" owner Joe and his "friendly" staff make the enterprise "fun."

Joe's on the Green ⑤   – | – | – | M

Kiahuna Golf Course, 2545 Kiahuna Plantation Dr., Poipu,
808-742-9696

With the same great breakfasts, lunches and Thursday night dinners and the same great owner as Joe's Courtside Cafe, this open-air Cal-American serves filling fare in a laid-back, casual setting that overlooks the rolling greens of the Poipu golf course.

Kalaheo Coffee Co. & Cafe ⑤   22 | 14 | 20 | $13

2-2436 Kaumualii Hwy. (Papalina Rd.), Kalaheo,
808-332-5858

■ "Wonderful" homemade muffins and pastries ("two words: cinnamon knuckles"), tasty sandwiches and plenty of vegetarian options lure regulars to this "secret" "little" art-filled coffee shop in the heart of Kalaheo; though it doesn't serve dinner, it's just the ticket for a "fast", "healthy" breakfast or lunch.

Kalaheo Steak House ⑤   21 | 15 | 21 | $24

4444 Papalina Rd., Kalaheo, 808-332-9780

■ "Great bargain steaks" are the lure at this dinner-only Kalaheo surf 'n' turfer, which also draws applause for its "nice" staff; but insiders advise arriving early, since it "fills up fast" with "lots of locals."

Keoki's Paradise ⑤   22 | 25 | 21 | $27

Poipu Shopping Village, 2360 Kiahuna Plantation Dr.
(Poipu Rd.), Poipu, 808-742-7534

■ A "tropical Disneyland environment", replete with "waterfalls", "lagoons" and "live Hawaiian music", attracts "tourists", "twentysomethings" and "kids" to this "fun", "upbeat" Poipu steakhouse-seafooder ("Don the Beachcomber eat your heart out"); though it might be "too noisy for old folks", "this place grows on you."

Kokee Lodge S
13 | 15 | 13 | $14
Kokee State Park, 3600 Kokee Rd., Waimea, 808-335-6061

■ Before a morning hike through Waimea Canyon, stock up on some decent sandwiches, salads and a slice of *lilikoi* pie at this "simple", "handy" coffee shop in the cool hills of Kokee State Park; pragmatists stress that this is the "only restaurant" in the area and only open for breakfast and lunch.

La Cascata S
∇ 23 | 22 | 20 | $48
Princeville Hotel, 5520 Ka Haku Rd., Princeville, 808-826-2761

◪ Dine on "solid" Italian cuisine while taking in earth-toned murals, a fountain and a "beautiful view of Hanalei Bay" at this elegant if "expensive" Princeville venue; a few party poopers sigh it's "not what it used to be", however.

Mema Thai Chinese Cuisine S
∇ 25 | 20 | 21 | $21
4-361 Kuhio Hwy. (Kinipopo Shopping Village), Kapaa, 808-823-0899

■ "Don't miss" this taste of Bangkok with "wonderful Thai" decor "hidden" away in Kapaa; fans praise "awesome" dishes like the signature curry with kaffir lime leaves, lemongrass, garlic and coconut milk.

Ono Family Restaurant S
23 | 17 | 21 | $15
4-1292 Kuhio Hwy., Kapaa, 808-822-1710

■ Kauaians are crazy about this Kapaa coffee shop that's "da best" when it comes to "excellent" breakfasts and lunches; it's "onolicious", particularly if you have a yen for "huge omelets", "great burgers" or some of the "best black bean soup on the island."

Pattaya Asian Cafe S
22 | 16 | 20 | $21
Poipu Shopping Village, 2360 Kiahuna Plantation Dr. (Poipu Rd.), Poipu, 808-742-8818

◪ Surveyors have mixed emotions about this Thai-focused Asian in Poipu: fans praise the "great variety of tastes" while foes call it a "real disappointment", yet there is some agreement that one is at "the mercy of the wind" when dining in its "outdoor lanai setting."

Piatti S
25 | 25 | 23 | $35
Kiahuna Plantation Resort, 2253 Poipu Rd. (next to Sheraton Hotel Kauai), Poipu, 808-742-2216

■ Located in a "former plantation owner's" lava rock house in Koloa that sports cherrywood floors, rattan ceiling fans and a lanai overlooking "beautiful" gardens and koi ponds, this "romantic" Italian supplies "excellent", "high-style" cuisine complemented by an extensive wine list; overall, it's a true "hidden surprise."

Plantation House of Poipu ⑤ 22 | 20 | 20 | $24
Poipu Shopping Village, 2360 Kiahuna Plantation Dr.
(Poipu Rd.), Poipu, 808-742-7373
■ "Tucked back in the corner" of the Poipu Shopping Village
is this three-meals-a-day American with "plantation-style"
decor and a "great selection of sandwiches, pizzas",
fried chicken and the like; admirers say it's definitely
"worth looking for."

Pomodoro Ristorante Italiano ⑤ 24 | 18 | 24 | $26
Rainbow Plaza, 2-2514 Kaumualii Hwy., Kalaheo,
808-332-5945
■ "Old-style" Kalaheo Italian offering "excellent" if "basic"
fare in "generous portions" at "reasonable prices"; a
"very friendly staff" and "nice owners" make this "small",
"intimate" spot a local "favorite."

Postcards Cafe ⑤ ▽ 21 | 20 | 22 | $24
5-5075A Kuhio Hwy., Hanalei, 808-826-1191
■ In a "cute" little house on the edge of Hanalei lies this
Vegetarian serving upscale omelets, hotcakes and fresh
fruit plates at breakfast and a full lineup of "healthy" and
"creative" fare for dinner (including some fish dishes);
"pleasant service" and a "relaxed atmosphere" ice the
cake, but bear in mind they don't do lunch.

Restaurant Kintaro 24 | 21 | 22 | $31
4-370 Kuhio Hwy., Kapaa, 808-822-3341
■ "Probably the best Japanese food on the island" cheer
fans of this family-owned Kapaa eatery, which propels
patrons into "teppanyaki heaven" and also provides them
with some of the "best sushi" around; expect "several
ways to dine", including a tatami room, a sushi bar and
American-style tables.

Roadrunner Bakery & Cafe ⑤ ▽ 19 | 14 | 15 | $16
2430 Oka St. (A'Aloma), Kilauea, 808-828-8226
■ Although this Kilauea Mexican is now under new
ownership, it still features the same "superb" fresh fish
tacos and flautas, handpainted murals and "value" prices
that it was previously known for; P.S. there's also a bakery
that produces breads, bagels, cakes and pastries.

ROY'S POIPU BAR & GRILL ⑤ 27 | 21 | 24 | $41
Poipu Shopping Village, 2360 Kiahuna Plantation Dr.
(Poipu Rd.), Poipu, 808-742-5000
☑ "You can always rely on" überchef Roy Yamaguchi,
whose Poipu "trophy kitchen" turns out "awesome"-looking,
"imaginative" Eurasian–Pacific Rim fare in a "very busy"
"open-air" space; granted, things can be "hectic", "loud",
"rushed" and "pricey", but overall it remains one of the
"best places on the island" to "take guests" – and the
chocolate soufflé is still "out of this world."

Shells S   ▽ 22 | 22 | 20 | $30
*Sheraton Kauai Resort, 2440 Hoonani Rd. (Kapili Rd.),
Koloa, 808-742-1661*
■ Rising star Scott Lutey produces some seriously tasty
Pacific Rim cuisine – notably his award-winning crab and
avocado sushi with a mac nut crust and Thai curry sauce –
at this Poipu "oceanfront dining" room; if you're lucky, the
"nice view" might include whales frolicking in the sea.

Tahiti Nui S   ▽ 19 | 18 | 21 | $23
5134 Kuhio Hwy., Hanalei, 808-826-6277
■ Owner Louise Marston "always takes good care of"
her customers at this longtime Hanalei Pacific Rimmer
known for hosting "the best authentic luau on Kauai";
Tahitian-Hawaiian entertainment makes for a "different
but fun" experience.

Tidepools S   23 | 27 | 23 | $42
*Hyatt Regency Kauai, 1571 Poipu Rd., Poipu,
808-742-1234*
◪ Polynesian thatched huts arranged around a koi pond
form the "brilliant" Hawaiian village–like setting at this
"unique", open-air seafooder-steakhouse in a top Poipu
resort; even though "service can be up and down" and
it's on the "expensive" side, most call it "worthwhile"
for "special occasions."

Tip Top Motel Cafe & Bakery S   18 | 9 | 14 | $12
3173 Akahi St., Lihue, 808-245-2333
■ Ever a "local family favorite", this "classic" Japanese-
influenced Lihue coffee shop works best for "basic",
"economical" breakfasts ("pancake heaven") and lunches
featuring "the best oxtail soup on Kauai"; that said, some
outsiders "still don't get" its appeal.

Tomkats Grille S   17 | 16 | 18 | $16
5404 Koloa Rd., Koloa, 808-742-8887
■ For an "inexpensive" meal in a "rustic", partially
"open-air" setting, consider this Koloa American grill,
which specializes in sandwiches, burgers and exotic
brews; though it's "nice for a quick meal", folks not in a
hurry sniff it's "totally ordinary."

Wailua Marina Restaurant S   ▽ 21 | 14 | 17 | $20
*5971 Kuhio Hwy. (Wailua River), Wailua,
808-822-4311*
■ Overlooking the Wailua River, this cavernous, open-air
American seafooder is "the place" to go for "parties and
get-togethers" as it proffers "large portions" of "excellent",
"local-style" vittles; it's a "great family restaurant" as well
as a "Kauai tradition."

Waimea Brewing Company ⑤   17 | 19 | 17 | $19
9400 Kaumualii Hwy., Waimea, 808-338-9733
■ Even though it's the "good beer on tap" and "relaxing" atmosphere that draw a "young" crowd to this brewpub on the grounds of the Waimea Plantation Cottages, there's also an Eclectic menu with grazing items such as taro leaf goat cheese dip and ale-steamed shrimp.

Whalers Brewpub ⑤   17 | 23 | 17 | $22
Kauai Lagoons Resort, 3132 Ninini Point St., Lihue, 808-245-2000
☑ "Go during daylight" for the "unparalleled" views of Nawiliwili Bay and the Kauai Lagoons Golf Course at this Eclectic brewpub in Lihue; while the "fun beer sampler" gets good notices, the edibles seem to be an afterthought ("can't remember what we ate").

Zelo's Beach House ⑤   20 | 18 | 19 | $19
Ching Young Village, 5-8420 Kuhio Hwy. (Aku Rd.), Hanalei, 808-826-9700
■ A "colorful", ethnic art–filled old Hanalei beach house with a popular outdoor deck makes for a "fun" setting at this Pacific Rim seafooder, which offers "huge portions" off a "varied menu" that ranges from sandwiches, burgers and babybacks to more complex creations like crab-stuffed fish; even though it's "very busy", many call it the "perfect place for lunch."

Lanai

F	D	S	C

Blue Ginger Cafe ⑤⧥   17 | 12 | 15 | $13
409 Seventh St., Lanai City, 808-565-6363

■ Tiny, "funky" coffee shop in Lanai City that dishes out "typical" "local food" that's "hearty" but certainly "not fancy"; still, it "fills a need" when "you can't afford" the "luxury hotel alternatives."

Henry Clay's Rotisserie ⑤   23 | 18 | 21 | $32
Hotel Lanai, 828 Lanai Ave. (9th St.), Lanai City, 808-565-7211

■ This Cajun–New American in the 11-room Hotel Lanai is known for its "great game" and kiawe-grilled seafood, served in two "comfortable", wood-paneled dining rooms as well as on a wicker furniture–adorned lanai; spendthrifts say it's "worth the plane fare to get there."

LODGE AT KOELE, THE FORMAL DINING ROOM ⑤   27 | 28 | 27 | $56
Lodge at Koele, 1 Keomuku Hwy., Lanai City, 808-565-4580

■ "After a hard day of golf", reward yourself with dinner at this "memorable" Lanai City resort dining room, a "beautifully decorated", "romantic" "jewel box" offering truly "outstanding" New American dishes; though the tab is "very expensive" and you'll have to don a jacket, this is the "ultimate epicurean's delight" – and Lanai's Most Popular restaurant, not to mention No. 2 for Decor and Service in the state.

Lodge at Koele, The Terrace ⑤   22 | 23 | 23 | $36
Lodge at Koele, 1 Keomuku Hwy., Lanai City, 808-565-4580

■ "Unbeatable views" of immaculate, English-style gardens and a 35-foot 'great wall' with a six-foot fireplace are the atmospheric high points of this informal, three-meal-a-day Pacific Rim dining room in the Lodge at Koele; fans say the "first-class" "attention" makes them feel "so comfortable" here.

Manele Bay Hotel, Hulopo'e Court S   23 | 25 | 23 | $40
Manele Bay Hotel, 1 Manele Rd. (Hulopo'e Bay), Lanai City, 808-565-2290

■ "Wonderful in every way", this high-end Hawaiian Regional overlooking the ocean and the Manele Bay Hotel's swimming pool features "excellent cuisine" that starts the day off with a "great breakfast buffet"; though closed for lunch, it resumes in the evening with tempting dishes like guava-glazed chicken with Molokai sweet potatoes.

Manele Bay Hotel, Ihilani S   26 | 26 | 25 | $58
Manele Bay Hotel, 1 Manele Rd. (Hulopo'e Bay), Lanai City, 808-565-2296

■ No attention to detail is spared at this "elegant" Mediterranean in the Manele Bay Hotel (considered more formal than the Hulopo'e Court), where the well-spaced tables ensure the "most romantic dinner ever"; the "superb food" of chef Edwin Goto includes an interesting selection of cheeses and not-to-be-missed desserts, and though some sigh it's "desperately expensive", most feel it's "worth it."

Maui

TOP 3 FOOD RANKING

Restaurant	Cuisine Type
26 Anuenue Room	Hawaiian Regional
Waterfront	Continental
Sansei Seafood	Hawaiian-Japanese

F	D	S	C

ANUENUE ROOM   26 | 25 | 27 | $65

Ritz-Carlton Hotel, 1 Ritz-Carlton Dr., Kapalua, 808-669-6200
■ "Everything is top of the line" at this Kapalua resort Hawaiian Regional where "great chef" Craig Connole deftly mixes steak and seafood with local ingredients like seaweed, fern shoots and taro; a "knowledgeable staff" (voted No. 1 for Service in the state), an elegant plantation-style setting and sunset views further enhance this total "treat."

A Pacific Cafe S   24 | 21 | 22 | $40

Azeka Place II, 1279 S. Kihei Rd. (Lipoa Rd.), Kihei, 808-879-0069
Honokowai Marketplace, 3350 Honoapiilani Rd., Lahaina, 808-667-2800
◪ "A great mix" of "exotic" Hawaiian Regional–Pacific Rim flavors emerge from the display kitchens of chef Jean-Marie Josselin's shopping mall–based Honokowai and Kihei restaurants, where signature dishes include wok-charred mahi mahi and tiger-eye sushi; the only drawbacks: "slow service" and "overpriced" tabs.

A SAIGON CAFE S   26 | 13 | 20 | $20

1792 Main St. (bet. Kaniela & Nani Sts.), Wailuku, 808-243-9560
◪ "Where would we be without it?" ask admirers addicted to this Wailuku Vietnamese's "subtle", "light" fare that's easily "the best in the state"; though it's "hidden in plain sight" with "no sign out front" and "no decor", the service is "friendly" and the prices "very cheap."

Bay Club S   22 | 25 | 22 | $46

Kapalua Bay Hotel & Villas, 1 Bay Dr., Kapalua, 808-669-8008
■ Atmosphere buffs dub this open-air, oceanside seafooder "the best spot for a two-hour lunch on Maui" because of its impressive view of Kapalua Bay (not to mention the "awesome sunsets" later on); though penny-pinchers protest it's "too expensive", partisans praise its "great Cajun fish" and claim it's "still one of the best."

Bubba Gump Shrimp Company S   14 | 19 | 17 | $20

889 Front St. (Papalaua St.), Lahaina, 808-661-3111
See review in Oahu Directory.

Buzz's Wharf 🖪   18 | 18 | 18 | $30
Maalaea Boat Harbor (Hwy. 30), Wailuku, 808-244-5426
◪ Overlooking the yachts at Maalaea Harbor, this casual
International has been a local "watering hole" for "what
ails you" since 1964; though picky eaters say it's "getting
tired" and a "little pricey", many more pronounce this
"solid" spot a "perennial favorite."

Carelli's on the Beach 🖪   19 | 23 | 18 | $51
2980 S. Kihei Rd. (Kilohana St.), Kihei, 808-875-0001
◪ Solid scores but very mixed reviews sum up this Kihei
Italian; boosters stand up for the "beautiful" ocean view
that's among "Maui's finest" while bashers say it's "all
flash and no substance", a "snobby", "vastly overpriced"
"tourist trap" that caters to "famous tourists"; your call.

Casanova Italian Restaurant 🖪   20 | 16 | 18 | $27
1188 Makawao Ave. (Baldwin Ave.), Makawao,
808-572-0220
◪ Located in the tiny Upcountry town of Makawao, this
"dependable" Italian attracts a "younger crowd" with
its pies, pastas, focaccia and live entertainment; though
some brand it "not exceptional" and even "mediocre",
many locals call it an "imaginative" "favorite."

Charley's Restaurant 🖪   20 | 15 | 17 | $18
142 Hana Hwy., Paia, 808-579-9453
■ "Bring your appetite" to this "laid-back" American in
Paia, a postsurfing "gathering spot" for "excellent
breakfasts" of "filling" pancakes and omelets; night owls
award it "points for being open late" – which on Maui
means 10 PM.

Chart House 🖪   19 | 19 | 18 | $29
1450 Front St. (Fleming St.), Lahaina, 808-661-0937
100 Wailea Ike Dr. (near Wailea Alanui Dr.), Wailea,
808-879-2875
See review in Oahu Directory.

Cheeseburger in Paradise 🖪   16 | 18 | 15 | $15
811 Front St. (Lahainaluna Rd.), Lahaina, 808-661-4855
See review in Oahu Directory.

Chez Paul Restaurant   25 | 20 | 24 | $50
820 Olowalu Village, Lahaina, 808-661-3843
■ Enthusiasts are thrilled that recently installed chef
Patrick Callarec (ex Ritz-Carlton Kapalua) is now preparing
"exquisite", "luscious" Classic French cuisine at this
Provence-style "country oasis" in "out-of-the-way"
Olowalu, four miles south of Lahaina; sure, it might be
"expensive, but it's equal to many top mainland places."

Compadres 🖪   16 | 17 | 16 | $19
Cannery Mall, 1221 Honoapiilani Hwy., Lahaina, 808-661-7189
See review in Oahu Directory.

DAVID PAUL'S LAHAINA GRILL S   26 | 23 | 23 | $45
127 Lahainaluna Rd. (Front St.), Lahaina, 808-667-5117
■ "Fall in love with food again" at this "heavenly" Lahaina
New American set in two "art-filled" dining rooms; expect
"inventive" dishes (e.g. tequila shrimp and firecracker rice)
that will have your "taste buds screaming more, more, more"
as well as "delightful" service and live jazz on weekends – in
short, nothing less than a "magical evening."

Feast at Lele, The   – | – | – | VE
505 Front St., Lahaina, 808-667-5353
This extraordinary, upscale luau presented in a lovely
oceanside setting is the result of the Old Lahaina Luau
partners joining forces with chef James McDonald (pacific'O
and i'o); together, they have created an evening of song,
dance and chants of four Pacific islands (Hawaii, Tonga,
Tahiti and Samoa), accompanied by corresponding cuisines.

Ferraro's at Seaside S   ▽ 23 | 24 | 23 | $40
*Four Seasons Resort, 3900 Wailea Alanui Dr., Wailea,
808-874-8000*
■ "Everything is first class" at this Wailea Four Seasons
Italian, another contender for the "most romantic setting
on the island" thanks to a fresco-filled dining room, outdoor
terrace and a nightly classical music trio; while the evening
is geared toward adults, the children's menu at lunch is
suitable for families looking for a quick, casual meal.

Gerard's S   25 | 24 | 25 | $50
*Plantation Inn, 174 Lahainaluna Rd. (Wainee Ln.), Lahaina,
808-661-8939*
■ "Charming" chef Gerard Reversade's long-running,
dinner-only New French in Lahaina still garners lots of kudos
for the "most authentic" Gallic dishes on Maui, a "huge wine
list", "superb" service, a "lovely" Victorian-style dining room
and veranda overlooking a garden; it might be "expensive"
but overall you can expect a "wonderful evening."

Greek Bistro S   19 | 16 | 17 | $25
Kai Nani Village, 2511 S. Kihei Rd., Kihei, 808-879-9330
■ One of the few Greek restaurants on Maui, this open-
air, dinner-only bistro in a mall across from Kihei's Kamaole II
Beach Park serves "authentic" Hellenic dishes, as well as
some vegetarian and seafood offerings; fans feel there's
"something for everyone" at this "nice change of pace."

Hakone   24 | 23 | 24 | $38
*Maui Prince Hotel, 5400 Makena Alanui Dr., Makena,
808-875-5888*
■ "Treat" yourself to an "authentic" meal at this "pricey",
dinner-only Japanese in a posh Makena resort overlooking
the ocean; expect a full range of menu options, from sushi,
sukiyaki, tempura and miso soup to contemporary items
like the ostrich *katsu* (cutlet) with sweet and sour sauce.

Haliimaile General Store S   25 | 22 | 22 | $36 |
900 Haliimaile Rd., Haliimaile, 808-572-2666
■ "Worth the drive" to Haliimaile, chef/owner Beverly
Gannon's New American-Asian presents "excellent" dishes
like Szechuan-barbecued salmon, Hunan rack of lamb and
piña colada cheesecake in an "old country store" setting
"surrounded by pineapple fields"; it might be "noisy" and
located in "the middle of nowhere", but enthusiasts feel
this is "the best restaurant on Maui for the money."

Hard Rock Cafe S   16 | 21 | 16 | $19 |
*Lahaina Ctr., 900 Front St. (Papalaua St.), Lahaina,
808-667-7400*
See review in Oahu Directory.

Hotel Hana-Maui   18 | 21 | 19 | $41 |
Main Dining Room S
Hotel Hana-Maui, Hana Hwy., Hana, 808-248-8211 x133
◪ Intrepid visitors to remote Hana admit that this serene
Pacific Rim hotel eatery overlooking the ocean is "not
very exciting, but at the moment the only game in town"
when it comes to fine dining; and though critics carp this
old-timer (since 1946) is "not consistent" and "showing
wear", defenders loyally insist it's "hanging in."

Hula Grill S   21 | 24 | 20 | $29 |
*Whaler's Village, 2435 Kaanapali Pkwy., Lahaina,
808-667-6636*
◪ "Tourists" and locals concur that it's "perfect sitting
outside" nibbling *pupu*, listening to live music and watching
the sun set with your "toes in the sand" at this Hawaiian
Regional seafooder at Whaler's Village in Kaanapali, even if
a few critics cite "spotty service" and "not exceptional food."

i'o S   ▽ 22 | 23 | 19 | $44 |
*505 Shopping Ctr., 505 Front St. (Shaw St.), Lahaina,
808-661-8422*
■ Chef James McDonald's cooking keeps "getting better and
better" at this dinner-only Lahaina Pacific Rimmer where
his "very interesting menu" is prepared in an exhibition
kitchen; a martini bar and "beautiful" ocean view further
enhance this "perfect showcase" of "incredible dishes."

Jacques Bistro S   21 | 18 | 19 | $27 |
89 Hana Hwy. (Baldwin Ave.), Paia, 808-579-6255
Jacques on the Beach S
760 S. Kihei Rd., Kihei, 808-875-7791
■ Lauded as "Maui's best bargain", these Hawaiian-
influenced French bistros serve "simple, hearty" fare
along the lines of bouillabaisse, lamb and *ahi poke*; while
the original branch in the funky old sugar cane town of
Paia is "noisy" and "crowded", the newer outlet on the
water in Kihei might be a tad less frenetic.

Joe's Bar & Grill ⑤   20 | 18 | 20 | $39
Wailea Tennis Ctr., 131 Wailea Ike Pl., Wailea, 808-875-7767

■ Overlooking the Wailea Tennis Courts, this "charming" Traditional American from Haliimaile General Store owners Beverly and Joe Gannon proffers "great food" accompanied by "fun *pupu*"; it's certainly "more accessible" than their other eatery, and true believers think it's "somehow better."

Kea Lani Restaurant ⑤   ▽ 24 | 25 | 23 | $40
Kea Lani Hotel Suites & Villas, 4100 Wailea Alanui Dr., Wailea, 808-875-4100

■ A cooked-to-order omelet station adds some zip to the "yummy" breakfasts (the only meal served) at this open-air American cafe at a swank Wailea resort; "attentive" service and a poolside setting are other pluses.

Kimo's ⑤   19 | 22 | 19 | $29
845 Front St., Lahaina, 808-661-4811

■ "Lively", "old-time" Lahaina Hawaiian seafooder that's "always a safe bet" for a nice assortment of *pupu*, "big portions of prime rib" and a slice of hula pie (free for birthday celebrants); ocean views of "crashing waves" draw "lots of tourists" at this "always busy" spot.

Kobe ⑤   21 | 17 | 19 | $30
136 Dickenson St. (Front St.), Lahaina, 808-667-5555
See review in Oahu Directory.

Kula Lodge & Restaurant ⑤   18 | 22 | 18 | $26
Haleakala Hwy., Rte. 377, Kula, 808-878-1535

☒ Located 3,500 feet up the slope of the extinct volcano Haleakala, this "rustic", knotty pine–filled lodge offers its "captive audience" a "spectacular vista" of mountains, valleys, islands and the ocean beyond; while the "homey" Eclectic fare can be "unpredictable", it's a safe bet for breakfast or drinks at sunset.

Lahaina Coolers   ▽ 18 | 18 | 18 | $24
Restaurant & Bar ◐ ⑤
Dickenson Sq., 180 Dickenson St. (Front St.), Lahaina, 808-661-7082

■ On a side street in Lahaina lies this "laid-back" Eclectic "hangout" with "surfer decor" and an "inventive" menu of "fun" fare – evil jungle Thai pizza, fresh fish tacos – from a kitchen that stays open until midnight; P.S. the popular happy hour offers the opportunity to mix with locals.

Leilani's on the Beach ⑤   17 | 21 | 18 | $28
Whaler's Village, 2435 Kaanapali Pkwy., Kaanapali, 808-661-4495

■ "Another old standby" to take in "beautiful" ocean views over "drinks and *pupu*", this open-air cafe on Kaanapali Beach offers two menus: a selection of light fare (salads, sandwiches, plate lunches) served all day as well as a range of steakhouse options in the evening; however you approach it, save room for the "good desserts."

Longhi's ⑤ | 20 | 18 | 17 | $35 |
888 Front St. (Papalaua St.), Lahaina, 808-667-2286
☑ "Touristy", two-story Lahaina Italian-Mediterranean
with a "verbal menu" that inspires controversy: pros call
it a "fun presentation" but cons say they're "tired of" the
"irritating" recitation; otherwise, there's agreement on the
"expensive but good" food and the thrill of "watching LA
tourists on cell phones."

Makawao Steak House ⑤ | 19 | 19 | 20 | $29 |
3612 Baldwin Ave. (bet. Brewer St. & Makawao Ave.),
Makawao, 808-572-8711
☑ Those looking to try Upcountry *paniolo*-style fare should
gallop by this "dark", dinner-only steakhouse in off-the-
beaten-tourist-path Makawao; while the "basic", "steady"
offerings are "not spectacular", the atmosphere is "friendly"
enough to make you forget your last hotel meal.

MAMA'S FISH HOUSE ⑤ | 25 | 25 | 23 | $43 |
799 Poho Pl. (Hana Hwy.), Kuau, 808-579-8488
■ Set in a "drop-dead beautiful" former beach house with
Polynesian decor and an "excellent" ocean view ("this is the
fantasy we try to sell here in Hawaii"), this Kuau destination
is the "gold standard of seafood restaurants"; despite
being "touristy" and "a bit pricey", so many feel it "never
disappoints" that it's been voted the *Survey's* Most Popular
restaurant on Maui.

Marco's Grill & Deli ⑤ | 18 | 14 | 19 | $21 |
444 Hana Hwy. (Dairy Rd.), Kahului, 808-877-4446
☑ This conveniently located Kahului eatery is both an
"upscale grill" serving "big portions" of "consistent" Italian
fare as well as a "quick" service, "NY-style" deli with white
booths and black-tiled tables; though detractors complain
it gets "too noisy", most deem it a "solid" choice; N.B. a
new Kihei branch is scheduled to open in spring 2000.

Maui Tacos ⑤ | 18 | 11 | 14 | $11 |
Kaahumanu Ctr., 275 Kaahumanu Ave., Kahului, 808-871-7726
Kamaole Beach Ctr., 2411 S. Kihei Rd., Kihei, 808-879-5005
Lahaina Sq., 840 Wainee St. (Lahainaluna Rd.), Lahaina,
808-661-8883
Napili Plaza, 5095 Napilihau St., Napili, 808-665-0222
■ Some of the "best tacos" in Hawaii can be found at this
Mexican minichain featuring "great" veggie dishes and
"big" burritos served up "fast" at a "good price"; loyalists
say "they treat their customers right."

Milagros Food Company ⑤   ▽ | 19 | 17 | 17 | $17 |
3 Baldwin Ave. (Hana Hwy.), Paia, 808-579-8755
■ The outdoor patio of this Hawaiian-influenced Mexican
is a "great" place to "people watch" the characters walking
the streets of Paia; so kick back with a refreshing margarita
and some blackened *ahi taquito* and let the show begin.

Nick's Fishmarket S
24 | 26 | 26 | $52

Kea Lani Hotel Suites & Villas, 4100 Wailea Alanui Dr.,
Wailea, 808-879-7224

■ Whether you sit outside on the vine-covered terrace or in the "romantic" dining room, you can expect "superb" seafood from chef Michael Miho and "excellent" service from "waiters who are like magicians" at this "pricey" eatery in a high-end Wailea resort; fans gush it's "beyond compare" and simply one of "the best in Hawaii."

OLD LAHAINA LUAU S
22 | 29 | 25 | VE

1251 Front St. (Kapunakea St.), Lahaina, 808-667-1998

■ "Forget those big hotel productions" because the "best luau on Maui" just might be at this "grand" open-air retreat offering a spectacular Hawaiian show, a "terrific" staff and plenty of "authentic" dishes; indeed, there is so "much aloha" at this "well-produced" event that surveyors have awarded it the Top Decor score in the state.

Outback Steakhouse S
19 | 17 | 18 | $24

Kahana Gateway Shopping Ctr., 4405 Honoapiilani Hwy.
(bet. Hoohui St. & Hwy. 30), Lahaina, 808-665-1822
See review in Oahu Directory.

Pacific Grill S
▽ 21 | 20 | 20 | $33

Four Seasons Resort, 3900 Wailea Alanui Dr., Wailea,
808-874-8000

☑ "One of Maui's best eateries", this quiet American-Asian is both "pleasing in taste and sight" thanks to the efforts of chef Scott Fernandez; devotees pronounce it "excellent in every way", though tougher critics feel it "needs polish."

pacific'O S
22 | 23 | 20 | $40

505 Front St. (Shaw St.), Lahaina, 808-667-4341

■ "A near-perfect dining experience" rave admirers of this "gorgeous" Lahaina Hawaiian Regional, a "fabulous setting" in which to enjoy chef James McDonald's "inventive", "whimsical" cooking; add some "live jazz" and a staff that "tries hard" and it's plain why many say it "can't be beat."

Paia Fishmarket S
21 | 14 | 15 | $19

110 Hana Hwy., Paia, 808-579-8030

■ For "fresh island fish" at "bargain" prices, many Paians "highly recommend" this "rustic" seafood "sandwich shop", a surfer hangout where big wooden benches serve as tables; sure, it's a "hole-in-the-wall", but it definitely "fills a niche" and is great "when you're in a hurry."

Palm Court S
▽ 22 | 19 | 21 | $34

Renaissance Wailea Beach Resort, 3550 Wailea Alanui Dr.,
Wailea, 808-879-4900

■ Try to get a table on the tranquil, coconut tree–lined terrace overlooking a koi pond, a waterfall and the ocean at this dinner-only Kihei Mediterranean; habitués hint that its "great" seafood buffet (Tuesday and Friday) is the best bet.

Pauwela Cafe 🅢🔾   ▽ 19 | 11 | 16 | $14 |
*Pauwela Cannery, 375 W. Kuiaha Rd. (Luahine Pl.), Haiku,
808-575-9242*
■ Set in a secluded industrial building in Haiku, this brightly
colored health fooder is worth seeking out for chef Becky
Speere's "hearty" breakfasts and "interesting" lunches;
aficionados plead "don't change anything about this place."

Pioneer Inn 🅢   13 | 16 | 14 | $21 |
*Best Western Pioneer Inn, 658 Wharf St. (bet. Front &
Hotel Sts.), Lahaina, 808-661-3636*
◪ "Old memories" prompt nostalgic visits to this Lahaina
American set in the island's best-known inn, which dates
from 1901; though foodies may find the fare "disappointing",
the historical decor makes this worth checking out.

Plantation House 🅢   23 | 25 | 19 | $39 |
Kapalua Resort, 2000 Plantation Club Dr., Kapalua, 808-669-6299
■ A truly "killer" vista from a hill overlooking the Kapalua
golf links draws gasps ("oh, the view") at this "beautiful"
Hawaiian Regional–Mediterranean; under the direction of
chef Alex Stanislaw, the kitchen is "on the move upward."

Polli's Mexican Restaurant 🅢   17 | 15 | 18 | $18 |
1202 Makawao Ave., Makawao, 808-572-7808
■ For "decent, quick food after a surf session", head to this
"casual" Upcountry Mexican offering "consistent" grub at
"moderate prices"; though "no big deal, it still packs 'em in."

Prince Court 🅢   24 | 22 | 23 | $43 |
*Maui Prince Hotel, 5400 Makena Alanui Dr., Makena,
808-875-5888*
■ Garnering votes for the "best Sunday brunch buffet on
Maui" is this "elegant" resort dining room, which boasts
views of Makena Beach and Molokini; expect a "wonderful"
New Hawaiian menu nightly during the rest of the week.

ROY'S KAHANA BAR & GRILL 🅢   26 | 19 | 23 | $42 |
*Kahana Gateway Shopping Ctr, 4405 Honoapiilani Hwy.
(bet. Hoohui St. & Hwy. 30), Kahana, 808-669-6999*
■ Many say "the best thing about Maui" is Roy Yamaguchi's
"special-occasion" Kahana restaurant, which is "worth
every penny" thanks to its "creatively presented" Hawaiian
Regional–Eurasian cuisine; though it might "sound like
everyone has a megaphone", overall this "awesome"
spot "seldom disappoints."

ROY'S NICOLINA 🅢   26 | 21 | 23 | $41 |
*Kahana Gateway Shopping Ctr., 4405 Honoapiilani Hwy.
(bet. Hoohui St. & Hwy. 30), Kahana, 808-669-5000*
■ "Ditto" say fans of "another great Roy's" that helps
absorb "the overflow" from his Kahana sibling next door, but
more than stands on its own with superb Pacific Rim fare
(and 25 nightly specials); other bonuses include a patio and a
decibel level that allows you to "converse with each other."

RUTH'S CHRIS STEAK HOUSE [S]   26 | 20 | 23 | $42
Lahaina Ctr., 900 Front St. (Papalaua St.), Lahaina, 808-661-8815
See review in Oahu Directory.

Saeng's Thai Cuisine [S]   21 | 18 | 19 | $21
2119 Vineyard St., Wailuku, 808-244-1567
■ This "exotic" Thai nestled in a "pleasant garden" on a
quiet Wailuku street provides a soothing "escape" from the
outside world; among the many "very good" dishes are
the crispy mahi mahi and garlic vegetables with shrimp.

Sam Choy's Kahului [S]   21 | 18 | 19 | $27
Kaahumanu Ctr., 275 Kaahumanu Ave., Kahului, 808-893-0366
◪ "Huge portions" ("as big as" the eponymous owner) of
"reasonably priced" Hawaiian Regional cuisine are the
highlight of this Kahului branch of Sam Choy's dining empire;
while naysayers find the fare "uneven" and protest the
kitchen's "quantity not quality" approach, even fans wonder
"can it deliver on its big-time reputation?"

Sam Choy's Lahaina [S]   19 | 19 | 17 | $31
Lahaina Ctr., 900 Front St. (Papalaua St.), Lahaina, 808-661-3800
◪ Marine-themed decor and a garden exhibition kitchen set
the scene at this Lahaina Choy's, which hits the spot when it
comes to Hawaiian Regional favorites; foes find the service
"really slow" and opine it "needs more staff in the kitchen."

Sam Sato's ⇗   21 | 13 | 17 | $12
*Millyard Industrial Complex, 1750 Wili Pa Loop, Wailuku,
808-244-7124*
■ A Wailuku "institution" (since 1933), this "local-style"
Hawaiian exudes a blue-collar, "family-style ambiance"
that complements its no-nonsense "cheap" eats; some of
"Maui's best plate lunches" are available here, not to
mention some of the island's "favorite noodles."

SANSEI SEAFOOD   26 | 20 | 23 | $37
RESTAURANT & SUSHI BAR [S]
115 Bay Dr., Kapalua, 808-669-6286
■ D.K. Kodama's "out-of-this-world sushi" and "exciting",
"skillfully created" Hawaiian-Japanese cuisine, served by
an "excellent", "friendly" staff, make this dinner-only high-
achiever in the Shops at Kapalua a "favorite place to eat
in Maui"; in sum, it's "crowded because it's good."

Seasons   ▽ 25 | 28 | 26 | $63
*Four Seasons Resort, 3900 Wailea Alanui Dr., Wailea,
808-874-8000*
◪ Even though its former chef has left this "beautiful spot"
in the Wailea Resort for greener pastures in Honolulu, this
International is now showcasing the "wonderful" cuisine
of chef Pierre Albaladejo; so bring a big wallet and prepare
yourself for an evening of tantalizing tastes (available à la
carte or via three tasting menus), live island entertainment
and dancing on the terrace.

Seawatch Restaurant S   21 24 18 $36
Wailea Resort, 100 Wailea Golf Club Dr., Wailea,
808-875-8080
■ While this Hawaiian seafooder high atop a Wailea golf
course is recommended for breakfast and lunch (they're a
"better value" than dinner), surveyors admit you shouldn't
"miss the sunset" view of Molikini because it's "soooo
beautiful"; nonbelievers, however, say that "too many
chef changes" make for "inconsistent food."

Stella Blues Cafe & Deli S   17 13 15 $18
1215 S. Kihei Rd., Kihei, 808-874-3779
◪ Sure, three meals a day are served, but it's the pancakes,
omelets and bagels in the morning and "great sandwiches"
and salads at lunch that garner the most attention at this
"funky", Grateful Dead–themed Eclectic cafe in a Kihei
shopping center; the unimpressed yawn everything about
it is "unremarkable."

Swan Court S   25 26 24 $47
Hyatt Regency Maui, 200 Nohea Kai Dr. (Kaanapali Pkwy.),
Lahaina, 808-667-4727
■ You and the object of your affections will "love the
swans", musicians, waterfall and ocean view at this "oh
so romantic" dining room in a luxurious Kaanapali hotel;
the Pacific Rim cuisine is a "real treat" too, with special
kudos to the "excellent" Sunday breakfast buffet.

Tokyo Tei S   23 14 19 $16
Puuone Plaza, 1063 E. Lower Main St., Wailuku,
808-242-9630
■ "Outstanding shrimp tempura" heads up an impressive
menu of "local-style" Japanese dishes at this "family-
oriented", "secret" Wailuku eatery with "value" prices
and a real "mom-and-pop atmosphere"; one of the oldest
eateries on Maui, this venerable "standard" has been
around since 1937.

Tony Roma's S   19 14 17 $22
Kukui Mall, 1819 S. Kihei Rd. (Halama St.), Kihei,
808-875-1104
See review in Oahu Directory.

WATERFRONT RESTAURANT S   26 23 25 $44
50 Haouli St. (bet. Rtes. 30 & 31), Maalaea, 808-244-9028
■ "Inviting" Continental seafooder that's "excellent in all
categories" from its "very dependable" menu offering a
wide variety of "quality" fish and meat to its "European-
style" service and "wonderful view" of Maalaea Harbor;
in short, "one of the best restaurants on Maui."

Molokai

	F	D	S	C

Kanemitsu Bakery 🅂⊘   <u>18</u> <u>9</u> <u>16</u> <u>$10</u>
79 Ala Malama St., Kaunakakai, 808-553-5855
■ Admirers say this "no-atmosphere" Kaunakakai bakery/
cafe is an "institution" for the "best bread on the island"
and a good place to "meet locals" while taking in the
"flashback to the '30s" decor; do-it-yourself types advise
"buy the premade mix."

Maunaloa Room 🅂   <u>-</u> <u>-</u> <u>-</u> <u>E</u>
Molokai Ranch Lodge, Maunaloa Rd., Maunaloa, 808-660-2725
The recently opened Molokai Ranch Lodge in the cool
mountain area of Maunaloa features Traditional American
cooking in its cowboy-esque dining room with such creative
dishes as Molokai sweetbread French toast for breakfast,
ahi poke burger with wasabi mayonnaise for lunch and
pan-seared local venison for dinner; it may be Molokai,
but you can expect prices straight out of NYC.

Molokai Pizza Cafe 🅂⊘   ▽ <u>15</u> <u>11</u> <u>15</u> <u>$13</u>
Kahua Ctr., Kaunakakai, 808-553-3288
■ On an island with few restaurant options, many locals
are just plain "happy" for the mere existence of this Eclectic
Kaunakakai cafe, which offers everything from pizza,
sandwiches and pasta to fresh fish, Mexican vittles (on
Wednesday) and prime rib (on Sunday night); P.S. allow
some extra time to compensate for the "slow service."

Ohia Lodge Restaurant 🅂   ▽ <u>16</u> <u>16</u> <u>13</u> <u>$25</u>
*Kaluakoi Hotel & Golf Club, Kaluakoi Rd., Maunaloa,
808-552-2555*
☑ "Go for the sunset" to this West End American in the
Kaluakoi Resort overlooking Kepuhi Beach where popular
menu choices include the shrimp cocktail, Portuguese bean
soup and rack of lamb; Hawaiian entertainment (Friday–
Saturday night) provides appropriate tropical flair.

Village Grill 🅂   ▽ <u>16</u> <u>16</u> <u>16</u> <u>$20</u>
Maunaloa Hwy., Maunaloa, 808-552-0012
■ One of Molokai's newer eateries, this surf 'n' turfer in
an old plantation building in the cool country of Maunaloa
attracts "very friendly local patrons" to its antique bar
and wrap-around lanai; dishes range from fresh island
fish to big slabs of beef, along with some intriguing items
from the new stone grill.

Oahu

F	D	S	C

Aaron's Atop the Ala Moana ◑⑤　—｜—｜—｜E

Ala Moana Hotel, 410 Atkinson Dr. (bet. Ala Moana & Kapiolani Blvds.), Honolulu, 808-955-4466

Restaurateur Aaron Placourakis' latest features an American-Continental menu with Mediterranean influences courtesy of chef Todd Carlos (ex Lanai's Lodge at Koele); aside from being one of the few places to dine in Honolulu after midnight, it also boasts an 1,800-bottle wine cellar and stunning views from the top floor of the Ala Moana Hotel.

Acqua ⑤　19｜19｜19｜$35

Hawaiian Regent Hotel, 2552 Kalakaua Ave., 3rd fl. (bet. Ohua & Paoakalani Sts.), Honolulu, 808-924-0123

◪ Fans of this "exotic", "secret" Mediterranean–Pan Pacific on the third floor of a swank Waikiki hotel rave about the "well-prepared food" at a "good price", the "romantic" ocean view and the "pleasant" room; but service varies from "above average" to "substandard", and some are turned off by the "cavernous" space and "too casual" ambiance.

Ahi's Punaluu　14｜9｜15｜$15

53-146 Kamehameha Hwy. (north of the Crouching Lion), Punaluu, 808-237-8474

◪ Tucked way away on the Windward side, this "casual, island-style" eatery with "funky" decor dishes out cheap Hawaiian chow such as "excellent Kahuku shrimp" and "great fish" that's "very fresh"; though some say the "original [Kahuku site] was better", it's still "fun and very Hawaiian."

Akasaka ◑⑤　21｜13｜17｜$28

1646-B Kona St. (Kapiolani Blvd., behind Ala Moana Hotel), Honolulu, 808-942-4466

Akasaka Marina ⑤　18｜16｜15｜$27

Koko Marina Shopping Ctr., 7192 Kalanianoole Hwy. (bottom of Hanauma Bay), Honolulu, 808-396-4474

◪ The "best sushi in the world" attracts devotees to this "crowded" "hole-in-the-wall" near Ala Moana, but its "awful" location surrounded by "strip clubs" prompts some to "only do lunch" and steers others to the Koko Head branch with its "beautiful view of the Marina."

ALAN WONG'S ⑤   27 | 20 | 25 | $48
McCully Ct., 1857 S. King St. (bet. Hauoli & Pumehana Sts.), Honolulu, 808-949-2526

■ Voted Oahu's Most Popular restaurant as well as No. 1 for Food, this Pacific Regional boasts the "most creative chef in Hawaii", Alan Wong, who is simply "da man" of "innovative", "creative" cooking; despite a "crowded", "uninspired" room, the "exceptionally exceptional" (albeit "pricey") food and "imaginative presentations" make this an "event" for locals and a "must-go for out-of-towners."

Alfred's   24 | 20 | 23 | $37
Century Ctr., 1750 Kalakaua Ave., 3rd fl. (Kapiolani Blvd.), Honolulu, 808-955-5353

☑ "Those who desire a bit of the old world" appreciate the "consistent", "authentic" Continental-Swiss cuisine, "dark-wood decor", generally "excellent" service and "bargain" prices at this "mainstay" in a high-rise across from the Convention Center; although foes sigh it's "past its prime" and dub the windowless room "dark and dreary", it remains a "great hidden treasure" to its loyal clientele.

Andy's Sandwiches & Smoothies ⑤   21 | 8 | 19 | $8
2904 E. Manoa Rd. (Huapala St.), Honolulu, 808-988-6161

■ "Best meal for under $10 in the state: healthy, cheap and delicious" sums up Hawaii's No. 1 Bang for the Buck eatery, a "crowded little hole-in-the-wall" in Manoa serving "mile-high" sandwiches "worth waiting for" and some of the "best smoothies on the island"; N.B. closed Saturdays and after 5 PM on Fridays.

Angelo Pietro Honolulu ⑤   17 | 16 | 16 | $18
1585 Kapiolani Blvd., Honolulu, 808-941-0555

☑ "Sometimes it works, sometimes it doesn't" is the general consensus on this Italian-Japanese "hybrid" (part of a trend in recent years) that is either "innovative" or "strange", an "outstanding value" or "expensive for the portions"; voters tend to agree on its "interesting", "eclectic" decor and service "with a smile", however.

A Pacific Cafe ⑤   22 | 21 | 20 | $37
Ward Ctr., 1200 Ala Moana Blvd. (bet. Piikoi St. & Ward Ave.), Honolulu, 808-593-0035

☑ Though many remark that chef Jean-Marie Josselin's top-rated Kauai branch "is much better", most also agree that this Ward Centre sibling delivers some "creative" (and "pricey") Pacific Rim delicacies that "appeal to both the stomach and the soul"; but while ratings suggest it's "better than most", "disappointed" dissenters insist it "doesn't meet the hype" and find both food and service "hit and miss"; the "funky" art deco decor similarly has its friends and foes.

Assaggio ⑤   21 | 17 | 19 | $24
Koko Marina Shopping Ctr., 7192 Kalanianoole Hwy.
(bottom of Hanauma Bay), Honolulu, 808-396-0756
Mililani Town Shopping Ctr., 95-1249 Meheula Pkwy.
(opp. Star Market), Honolulu, 808-623-5115
354 Uluniu St. (Auliki), Kailua, 808-261-2772
☑ "The perfect neighborhood eatery" rave fans of this
suburban "house of garlic", a minichain offering "big
portions" of "good Americanized Italian food" (e.g. "divine"
Caesar salads) in "comfortable" atmospheres with "first-
rate" service; of course, they're "not in the top echelon",
but they are a "good bargain" all the same.

Auntie Pasto's ⑤   17 | 12 | 16 | $16
1099 S. Beretania St. (Pensacola St.), Honolulu,
808-523-8855
☑ Overcoming its location near Ala Moana, this "authentic
Italian hole-in-the-wall" has a "neighborhoody" feel, drawing
the "college crowd" and "families" with "hearty" mounds
of "decent, cheap" pasta; despite "no parking", a "crowded,
noisy" setting and "amazingly long waits in line", it endures,
although foes grumble "you get what you pay for."

Azteca   16 | 10 | 16 | $16
3617 Waialae Ave. (12th Ave. & Koko Head), Honolulu,
808-735-2492
☑ Although amigos of this tiny, family-run Kaimuki Mexican
call it a "jewel", citing its "good, honest" chow and "cozy,
friendly" ambiance, bashers insist it's "ok, but not like it
used to be" and complain about "ho-hum" cooking and
"small, dingy" digs; your call.

Azul   22 | 24 | 22 | $55
JW Marriott Ihilani Resort & Spa, 92-1001 Olani St.,
Kapolei, 808-679-0079
☑ Hidden in the hinterlands of West Oahu lies this "elegant"
resort dining room where admirers say chef Randall Ishizu
prepares Mediterranean cuisine that achieves "absolute
perfection"; a "great wine selection" and "truly attentive
staff" draw even more huzzahs, yet despite all this quality,
many still feel it's "way overpriced"; N.B. dinner only,
Monday, Wednesday, Friday and Saturday.

Baci Bistro ⑤   22 | 17 | 20 | $30
30 Aulike St. (Kailua Rd.), Kailua, 808-262-7555
☑ "Everything on the menu is worth ordering" at this
"charming neighborhood place" in Kailua, where the
"addictive" Italian fare is "pricey but good" and includes
some of the "best bruschetta on the islands"; service is
"mostly friendly" (though it can be "undependable"), and
those who find the small dining room "noisy" can take
refuge on the outdoor patio.

Ba-Le French Sandwich & Bakery   18 | 6 | 14 | $8
377 Keahole St., Honolulu, 808-396-6556
801 Alakea St., Honolulu, 808-545-2221
Nimitz Airport, 3131 N. Nimitz Hwy., Honolulu, 808-836-1668 🅂 🍴
2242 Kamehameha Hwy., Honolulu, 808-847-4600 🍴
Kahala Mall, 4211 Waialae Ave., Honolulu, 808-735-6889 🅂 🍴
333 Ward Ave., Honolulu, 808-591-0935
Fort St. Mall, 1154 Fort St. (First Hawaiian Tower),
Honolulu, 808-521-4117 🍴
150 N. King St., Honolulu, 808-521-3973 🅂 🍴
Ala Moana Ctr., 1450 Ala Moana Blvd., Honolulu,
808-944-4752
Pearlridge Shopping Ctr., 98-180 Kamehameha Hwy., Aiea,
808-487-7280
Additional locations throughout Oahu.
■ "Dependable and ubiquitous" Vietnamese fast-fooders that just might be "the best l'il sandwich shops in the Sandwich Islands", thanks to their "crispy" French rolls and "great pho"; granted, they're "nothing fancy", but they are "quick", "somewhat healthy" and offer good "value for your dollar."

Bali-By-The-Sea   23 | 25 | 24 | $47
Hilton Hawaiian Village, 2005 Kalia Rd. (Ala Moana Blvd.),
Honolulu, 808-941-2254
■ One of the islands' top "impress-your-date" restaurants, this "elegant yet comfortable" dining room in a "romantic" Waikiki Beach locale specializes in "excellent" Eurasian cuisine with a Hawaiian accent courtesy of chef Jean Luc Voegele; despite a few doubters ("a lot of hype"), most agree that the "super wine list and steward", "classy decor" and "great service" add up to an experience that's simply "the best for special occasions."

Beau Soleil   20 | 17 | 18 | $27
3184 Waialae Ave. (bet. 3rd & 4th Aves.), Honolulu,
808-732-0967
☑ The "pleasingly idiosyncratic" decor delights aesthetes at this "small" Kaimuki Mediterranean-French bistro where the "flavorful" but "limited" offerings change daily; the BYO policy (a rarity in Hawaii) makes it an "affordable" "gem" to fans, but dissenters gripe about "overrated" cooking, "slooow service" and "lousy parking" (hint: look for a space across from 4th Avenue).

Benihana 🅂   19 | 18 | 19 | $30
Hilton Hawaiian Village, 2005 Kalia Rd. (Ala Moana Blvd.),
Honolulu, 808-955-5955
☑ "Go for the show" of flashing knives as "fun" chefs with "amazing dexterity" slice, dice and cook your food tableside at this Waikiki Japanese; it's "great entertainment" "for visitors" and "kids", but the blasé deride "the same menu for 25 years" at this "smoky" "tourist trap."

Big City Diner - Kaimuki ●⑤   16 | 13 | 17 | $14
3565 Waialae Ave. (bet. 11th & 12th Aves.), Honolulu, 808-738-8855

☑ Families flock to this "late-night" Kaimuki diner with a "'50s rock 'n' roll" feel for its "big portions" of "affordable" Hawaiian "comfort food" like guava BBQ ribs and kimchee fried rice that "broke da mouth", the ultimate compliment.

Big Island Steak House ⑤   17 | 18 | 17 | $25
Aloha Tower Mktpl., 1 Aloha Tower Dr. (Bishop St.), Honolulu, 808-537-4446
See review in Big Island Directory.

Boston's North End Pizza Bakery ⑤⊘   18 | 7 | 13 | $10
98-302 Kamehamelia Hwy., Aiea, 808-487-5165
29 Hoolai St., Kailua, 808-263-7757
3506 Waialae Ave. (10th St.), Kaimuki, 808-734-1945
45-568 Kamehameha Hwy. (Duncan Dr.), Kaneohe, 808-235-7756
92-585 Makakilo Dr., Kapolei, 808-672-5566

☑ Pie partisans say you "can't beat the price and the portions" at this chain pizzeria, with special kudos to the "so tasty" spinach-garlic rendition and the "killer" calzones; detractors dis the "surly" service and "dingy" digs, adding that their business "would double with music half as loud."

Brew Moon ●⑤   17 | 22 | 17 | $22
Ward Ctr., 1200 Ala Moana Blvd. (Kamakee St.), Honolulu, 808-593-0088

☑ Conveniently located in Ward Centre, this "trendy watering hole" keeps microbrew mavens amused with its "interesting fluids" (including "homemade root beer") dispensed in an "attractive", "upbeat" setting; but "slow service" and a "clonish" New American menu leaves others "not impressed", dubbing it "all concept, no substance."

Bubba Gump Shrimp Company ⑤   14 | 19 | 17 | $20
Ala Moana Shopping Ctr., 1450 Ala Moana Blvd.
(bet. Atkinson Dr. & Piikoi St.), Honolulu, 808-949-4867

☑ Inspired by *Forrest Gump,* this "hokey" seafood chain fails to impress fin fans who say it "needs work", pointing to the "boring", "disappointing" eats ("too much shrimp") and way "too perky" staff; still, optimists insist it's "great for family dining", adding "you gotta be young to appreciate it."

Buzz's Original Steakhouse ⑤   18 | 17 | 17 | $24
413 Kawailoa Rd., Kailua, 808-261-4661 ⊘
98-751 Kuahao Pl., Pearl City, 808-487-6465

■ An "irresistible, laid-back" ambiance reminiscent of "1950s Hawaii" lures both locals and tourists to these "old standby" surf 'n' turfers that are renowned for their "classic salad bars" as well as "great steaks and mai tais"; the "fun and funky" Kailua branch seems to be the most popular of the pair, owing to its "location, location, location."

Cafe Che Pasta
19 | 17 | 17 | $20 |

Bishop Sq., 1001 Bishop St., Honolulu, 808-524-0004

■ "For fast business luncheons", zip by this Contemporary Italian whose "flavorful" cooking draws regulars who can't help but note there's "not much choice in Downtown Honolulu"; a "great renovation" has "made it look better", reflected in an all-around uptick in its ratings.

Cafe Haleiwa ⑤
19 | 13 | 16 | $13 |

66-460 Kamehameha, Haleiwa, 808-637-5516

■ "Laid-back", "funky" North Shore Cal-Mexican that's popular with waves of "surfers" hankering for "huge portions" of "the best breakfast on the island"; its "hang loose" atmosphere and "cheap" tabs keep the trade brisk, but bear in mind it stops serving at 2 PM.

Cafe Laufer ⑤
22 | 15 | 17 | $13 |

3565 Waialane Ave. (bet. 11th & 12th Aves.), Honolulu, 808-735-7717

■ The "best (and most fattening) desserts in town" weigh in at this "cozy" Kaimuki coffee shop that also delivers a "wonderful Chinese chicken salad"; a "cozy", "European" setting and "nice staff" are other pluses, though nitpickers find the prices just a little "too high."

Café Miró ⑤
23 | 16 | 20 | $33 |

3446 Waialae Ave. (9th Ave.), Honolulu, 808-734-2737

■ Formerly "a secret spot" that's now "caught on", this "charming" Kaimuki Contemporary French cafe offers a "small" prix fixe menu (the best way to order) that includes some "interesting fusion" choices; this former BYO now has a liquor license, yet everyone agrees that dinner is still a "great value."

Cafe Monsarrat ⑤
20 | 19 | 17 | $26 |

3106 Monsarrat Ave. (Kanaina Ave.), Honolulu, 808-737-6600

◪ In the shadow of Diamond Head, this Eclectic newcomer delivers tropical island fare in tapas-style, "small appetizer portions", meant to be "shared" by the entire table; though a few find the cooking "inconsistent", the room "too noisy" and the service "not up to par", many others say this "promising" "jewel" is a "great addition to the local scene."

Cafe Sistina ⑤
21 | 22 | 18 | $26 |

First Interstate Bldg., 1314 S. King St. (bet. Keeaumoku & Piikoi Sts.), Honolulu, 808-596-0061

■ "Michelangelo goes to Honolulu" at this Northern Italian notable for its "original murals" (adapted from the Sistine chapel) executed by chef Sergio Mitrotti, a "great painter and cook"; while most agree his "personal touch makes this place", a few request that he "go easy on the oil" – referring to his cooking, one assumes.

California Beach Rock n' Sushi S   19 | 14 | 17 | $20 |
404 Ward Ave. (Halekawila St.), Honolulu, 808-597-8000
■ "Rock 'n' roll with sushi" is the formula at this "hip"
Japanese near Ala Moana where the raw fish is offered
in "innovative", "nontraditional" presentations; though
you might "need to be in the mood" for the "pretty loud"
music, most praise the "happy atmosphere" and sum it
up as a "lot of fun."

California Pizza Kitchen S   19 | 16 | 17 | $17 |
Pearlridge Ctr., 98-1005 Moana Loa Rd., Aiea, 808-487-7741
Ala Moana Shopping Ctr., 1540 Ala Moana Blvd.
(Kapiolani Blvd.), Honolulu, 808-941-7715
Kahala Mall, 4211 Waialae Ave., Honolulu, 808-737-9446
■ "Consistent" if "predictable" "gourmet pizzas", pastas
and salads are served at this "upbeat" "high-end chain"
that fans flock to for both "good value" and "friendly"
service; some say "the portions seem to be getting smaller",
and no one likes the "long lines", but ultimately the verdict is
it's "worth the wait."

Cascada S   23 | 24 | 22 | $37 |
Royal Garden Hotel, 440 Olohana St. (bet. Alawai Blvd. &
Kuhio Ave.), Honolulu, 808-945-0270
■ "A surprising oasis in Waikiki", this New American
exudes romance thanks to "one of the loveliest dining
rooms in Hawaii", overlooking both a pool and a "relaxing
waterfall"; new chef Matt Stephenson completes the
"pleasant dining experience" with an "expensive", "very
well-done menu" that early visitors pronounce "superb."

Chai's Island Bistro S   23 | 23 | 21 | $31 |
Aloha Tower Mktpl., 1 Aloha Tower Dr. (Bishop St.),
Honolulu, 808-585-0011
■ "Wow!" rave fans, this Downtown Hawaiian Regional
is "da best of da best" of the Aloha Tower eateries: credit
chef Chai Chaowasaree's "intriguing menu" (that's so
"attractively presented" that it "needs to be photographed"),
a staff "willing to go the extra mile" and "great musical
entertainment", all presented in a "beautiful, relaxed
atmosphere"; the sole drawback – "parking that's not the
greatest" – scarcely detracts from this "definite repeat."

Chart House S   19 | 19 | 18 | $29 |
1765 Ala Moana Blvd. (Hobron Ln.), Honolulu, 808-941-6669
46-336 Haiku Rd., Kaneohe, 808-247-6671
◪ "The setting is everything" at this steakhouse duo, either
the "sunset" view "overlooking [Ala Wai] Yacht Harbor"
in Waikiki or the " spectacularly beautiful" Haiku Gardens
in Kaneohe; as for the food, diners praise the "great"
prime rib, fresh fish and desserts, though the "skimpy and
boring" salad bar draws yawns; N.B. the Waikiki branch
is independently owned.

Cheeseburger in Paradise ●⑤ | 16 | 18 | 15 | $15 |
Foster Tower, 2500 Kalakaua Ave. (Kealohilani), Honolulu, 808-923-3731
☑ Patty partisans love the "fun outdoor setting" of the Waikiki branch of this burger chain that offers "calorie busters" along the lines of "great cheeseburgers", steak fries and coleslaw, though dissenters call them "overpriced" and "overrated"; N.B. best bet for parking is on the street near the zoo.

Chef Mavro's ⑤ | 23 | 23 | 24 | $62 |
1969 S. King St. (McCully St.), Honolulu, 808-944-4714
☑ "Serious food for serious diners" comes courtesy of chef George Mavrothalassitis (ex La Mer, Seasons at Four Seasons Maui) at this "superior" McCully French–Hawaiian Regional, where the "fabulous food and wine pairings" draw huzzahs; sure, it's "expensive with a capital E" and hearty eaters groan that the servings are "microscopic", but to its many fans, this "must-try" spot is simply "ahead of its time."

Chiang Mai ⑤ | 22 | 18 | 18 | $19 |
2239 S. King St. (Makahiki Way), Honolulu, 808-941-1151
■ "Well-prepared", "authentic" dishes excite enthusiasts of this "cozy" Thai near Ala Moana known for its "large selection" and "reasonable prices"; though a few find the kitchen "erratic" and grumble about "uncomfortable" seating, far more laud its "consistent quality."

China House ⑤ | 17 | 12 | 12 | $18 |
Ala Moana Shopping Ctr., 1349 Kapiolani Blvd. (bet. Keeaumoku & Piikoi Sts.), Honolulu, 808-949-6622
■ Chinese in an Ala Moana shopping mall that most agree is "best for dim sum"; though "indifferent service" and "problem parking" turn off faultfinders, penny-pinchers plug the "awesome" buffet dinner that proffers "lots of food for the cost."

Chowder House ⑤ | 14 | 12 | 14 | $14 |
Ward Warehouse, 1050 Ala Moana Blvd. (Ward Ave.), Honolulu, 808-596-7944
☑ For a "cheap", "quick lunch", this American seafooder in Ward Warehouse comes across with "thick chowder" and "good fish sandwiches"; but many say this "dated" joint "could use some new recipes", not to mention a face-lift in the decor department.

Ciao Mein ⑤ | 21 | 21 | 20 | $32 |
Hyatt Regency Waikiki, 2424 Kalakaua Ave., Honolulu, 808-923-2426
☑ A Chinese-Italian fusion menu makes for a "unique dining experience" at this Waikiki hotel eatery where the "nice presentation" and "friendly service" win converts; the unconvinced, however, dismiss it as a "silly concept" – "some foods are just not meant to be married."

Coffee Gallery   15 | 15 | 12 | $9
*North Shore Shopping Mall, 66-250 Kamehameha Hwy.,
Haleiwa, 808-637-5355* S
800 Ft. Street Mall, Honolulu, 808-538-0032
■ "Put your Birkenstocks on before entering" these
"casual" coffee shops that make some feel like they're "still
in the '60s" (the "earthy" atmosphere is "so laid back it's
almost asleep"); still, "breakfast is a must" and java jivers
appreciate that they're "independent" from the other chains.

Compadres S   16 | 17 | 16 | $19
*Ward Ctr., 1200 Ala Moana Blvd., 3rd fl. (bet. Piikoi St. &
Ward Ave.), Honolulu, 808-591-8307*
☑ Surveyors are split on this Ward Centre Mexican,
with amigos admiring its "generous portions" served in a
"bustling" atmosphere with "views of Diamond Head" that
are enhanced by some "great margaritas"; but detractors
say this "pretty basic" "yuppie scene" is "consistently
mediocre" and advise it's "better just to drink" here.

Contemporary Museum Cafe S   20 | 20 | 17 | $16
2411 Makiki Heights Dr. (Mott Smith Dr.), Honolulu, 808-523-3362
■ Set in a "beautiful old Hawaii estate", this "often
overlooked" lunch-only museum cafe proffers "classy
American fare" on the slopes of Makiki Heights; its
"civilized", "relaxing" ambiance is "worth getting lost to find."

Diamond Head Grill S   – | – | – | E
*W Hotel, 2885 Kalakaua Ave. (Diamond Head), Honolulu,
808-922-3734*
In the space on the Kapiolani Park side of Waikiki that
formerly housed David Paul's Diamond Head Grill, chef
David Reardon (ex The Orchid at Mauna Lani) is now
dazzling fans with his version of Hawaiian Regional cuisine;
despite his impressive credentials and live entertainment
Tuesday–Saturday, the room hasn't caught fire – yet.

Dixie Grill Bar-B-Que &   16 | 16 | 16 | $18
Crab Shack S
404 Ward Ave. (Halekawila St.), Honolulu, 808-596-8359
☑ "Y'all come" to this "yummy" Southern BBQ near Ala
Moana, where there's "no class" and "nothing healthy
on the menu", just "really tender" ribs at "reasonable
prices"; it's "not a place for introverts" (everyone's
"loud and rowdy") and you can "expect to get messy",
but you'll "walk out satisfied."

Donato's Ristorante   22 | 18 | 18 | $33
4614 Kilauea Ave. (Pahoa Ave.), Honolulu, 808-738-5655
☑ "Fantastic", "authentic" Italian in a space near Kahala
Mall that specializes in thinly sliced raw meat and seafood;
though "small portions" at "expensive" prices and "slow
service" draw knocks, most find this "sophisticated" spot to
be "outstanding" and credit "master chef" Donato Loperfido.

Don Ho's Island Grill ◑ⓈＳ　　　12 | 18 | 14 | $22
Aloha Tower Mktpl., 101 Aloha Tower Dr. (Bishop St.),
Honolulu, 808-528-0807

◪ If you're in the mood for a "retro tiki" "'60s atmosphere"
along with "harborside tables" and "great live music",
this Aloha Tower Hawaiian Regional (named after the
island crooner famed for his rendition of *Tiny Bubbles)* fits
the bill; however, bubble-bursters sneer there's "nothing
interesting on the menu" at this "tacky" "tourist trap."

Duc's Bistro Ⓢ　　　24 | 19 | 21 | $32
1188 Maunakea St. (Beretania St.), Honolulu, 808-531-6325

◼ A "hidden treasure" in a "tough part of town", this
Chinatown French-Vietnamese offers "excellent food not
duplicated anywhere else" complemented by "bend-over-
backwards service"; fans "love the piano music" and say
this "low-key", "unpretentious" place is "very romantic" –
"the lighting makes everyone look good."

Duke's Canoe Club ◑Ⓢ　　　18 | 23 | 18 | $24
Outrigger Waikiki, 2335 Kalakaua Ave. (Kanekapole St.),
Honolulu, 808-922-2268

◼ The draw at this "hugely popular" American cafe (named
for swimmer Duke Kahanamoku, Hawaii's only Olympic
champ) is its "great view" of Waikiki; expect good "beach
people–watching", lots of Old Hawaiiana, an "impressive
salad bar" but otherwise only "ok food."

Eastern Garden Chinese Ⓢ　　　20 | 16 | 15 | $18
Westridge Ctr., 98-150 Kaonohi St. (opp. Liberty Hse.),
Aiea, 808-486-8882
Aston Waikiki Terrace, 2045 Kalakaua Ave., Honolulu,
808-951-8886
3008 Waialae Ave. (1st Ave.), Honolulu, 808-737-2828
46-023 Kamehameha Hwy., Kaneohe, 808-235-1628

◼ "You get your money's worth" at this "quality" Asian trio
"where the Chinese eat Chinese"; look for "mouthwatering
dim sum" as well as Cantonese and Hong Kong specialties,
all served in "friendly atmospheres."

Eggs 'n Things Ⓢ∅　　　23 | 12 | 19 | $12
1911-B Kalakaua Ave. (McCully St.), Honolulu, 808-949-0820

◼ "Big omelets" make for "big lines" at this "classic"
Waikiki "breakfast-only" joint that "opens in the middle of
the night" (11 PM) and closes at 2 PM; night owls like the
"colorful" wee hours crowd, the "wide selection" of menu
items and try their best to "ignore the decor."

El Burrito Ⓢ∅　　　20 | 10 | 17 | $12
550 Piikoi St. (Kapiolani Ave.), Honolulu, 808-596-8225

◼ "Authentic Mexican" located in a BYO "hole-in-the-
wall" near Ala Moana, offering "inexpensive", "surprisingly
good" tacos, burritos, huevos rancheros and other "home-
cooked" dishes; a "friendly" atmosphere ices the cake.

Fook Yuen Seafood ◐Ⓢ   19 | 13 | 14 | $18
McCully Shopping Ctr., 1960 Kapiolani Blvd. (McCully St.),
Honolulu, 808-973-0168
■ Penny-pinchers praise the "affordable" lobster and
"bargain" buffet lunch at this Chinese located on the
second floor of a shopping center on the periphery of
Waikiki; though some deduct points for "uneven service",
its late-late hours (open till 3 AM) thrill night owls.

Genki Sushi Ⓢ   18 | 13 | 15 | $16
900 Kapahulu Ave. (Olu St.), Honolulu,
808-735-8889
Waiau Shopping Ctr., 98-450 Kamehameha Hwy., Pearl City,
808-485-0227
■ "If you like cheap sushi", check out this Japanese
duo noteworthy for their "novel" delivery system – via an
"assembly line" on a "conveyor belt"; though nitpickers
deride it as "robo sushi", these "extremely popular" spots
must be doing something right as there are frequent "long
waits"; N.B. a third location, in Kaneohe's Windward City
Mall, is due later this year.

Golden Dragon Ⓢ   24 | 23 | 22 | $35
Hilton Hawaiian Village, 2005 Kalia Rd. (Ala Moana Blvd.),
Honolulu, 808-946-5336
■ For Oahu's "consummate Chinese restaurant", look no
further than this "superb", "top-of-the-line" spot where
"exquisite" dishes like the "to-die-for" lobster curry with
fried *haupia* arrive in a "quiet", "beautiful" setting within
a prestigious Waikiki hotel; granted, it's "expensive", but
for "truly gourmet" cooking, this "class act" is worth it.

Gordon Biersch Ⓢ   17 | 19 | 16 | $22
Aloha Tower Mktpl., 101 Ala Moana Blvd. (Nimitz Hwy.),
Honolulu, 808-599-4877
■ Ok, the food might "need a boost" at this Aloha Tower
Eclectic, but the "varied beer lineup" and "hot, tasty garlic
fries" make this microbrewery a favorite after-work
"watering hole"; "a great harbor view" and a "nice patio"
are other pluses, but "not enough help" detracts.

Grace's Drive Inn Ⓢⵝ   14 | 7 | 12 | $8
98 820 Moanalua Rd. (Kaahele St.), Aiea,
808-484-2028
Market City, 2919 Kapiolani Blvd. (bet. Harding & Kaimuki Aves.),
Honolulu, 808-732-0041
1296 S. Beretania St. (bet. Keeamoku & Piikoi Sts.),
Honolulu, 808-593-2202
■ Locals say this trio is just plain "heaven" when it comes to
its plate lunch and "good chicken katsu"; everything's
"cheap and fast", and portions are "generous" – "nothing
more, nothing less."

Hakone S   23 | 21 | 20 | $35
Hawaii Prince Hotel Waikiki, 100 Holomoana St.
(Ala Moana Blvd.), Honolulu, 808-956-1111
■ "Authentic" Japanese cooking, perhaps the "best in
town", can be found at this "expensive" Waikiki hotel eatery
overlooking the Ala Wai Yacht Harbor, where the lunch
buffet and sushi bar are "excellent"; N.B. lunch served
Tuesday–Friday only.

Hale Vietnam S   22 | 13 | 17 | $15
1140 12th Ave. (Waialae Ave.), Honolulu, 808-735-7581
■ Though this "busy, bustling" Kaimuki Vietnamese may
be "out of the way", it attracts wayfarers with a yen for
"something different"; some of the "best pho in town"
and an "abundance of fresh vegetables" are standouts on
its "large, ambitious menu."

Hanohano Room S   20 | 24 | 22 | $41
Sheraton Waikiki Hotel, 2255 Kalakaua Ave., 30th fl.
(bet. Lewers St. & Royal Hawaiian Ave.), Honolulu,
808-922-4422
◪ Up in the clouds on the 30th floor of the Sheraton Waikiki,
this "pricey" Asian seafooder's claims to fame are its
"spectacular" view and "fantastic Sunday brunch";
although nitpickers complain that the "food's not up to par"
with the stunning setting, most concur it's a "good choice
for business or romance"; N.B. breakfast and dinner only.

Hard Rock Cafe S   16 | 21 | 16 | $19
1837 Kapiolani Blvd. (Kalakaua Ave.), Honolulu,
808-955-7383
◪ "Enjoy the memorabilia" at this rock-themed chain
American – it's the "main attraction", not the "corporate
hamburgers" and other "so-so" eats; "loud", "blaring
music" makes it an option for "lunch with dull friends", but
ultimately voters shrug it's "best left to kids and tourists."

Harpo's Pizza S   16 | 11 | 14 | $12
Bishop Sq., 1001 Bishop St., Honolulu, 808-537-3439
Ala Moana Plaza, 451 Piikoi St., Honolulu, 808-591-0040
477 Kapahulu Ave. (Kanaina St.), Honolulu,
808-732-5525
Daiei Food Ct., 801 Kaheka, Kaheka, 808-943-8844
Windward Mall Food Ct., Kaneohe, 808-235-7595
Daiei Food Ct., Pearl City Shopping Ctr., Pearl City,
808-455-9044
◪ "When you need a quick bite", this ubiquitous Italian
chain pizzeria dishes out "yummy", "traditional" pies as
well as "tasty" veggie sandwiches and salads; some
complain that "service could be more pleasant", but there's
no argument that they're "dependable and convenient"
when you're "on the go."

Hau Tree Lanai **S**   20 | 25 | 19 | $29 |
New Otani Kaimana Beach Hotel, 2863 Kalakaua Ave.
(opp. Kapiolani Park), Honolulu, 808-921-7066
☑ Under a luxuriant hau tree in Waikiki lies this "beachside" American seafooder that many call nothing less than "true paradise"; though some quibble that the "enchanting" "location is better than the food", others aver it's "the best place for breakfast" – just beware of "flies on the buffet."

Hawaii Regional Cuisine   – | – | – | I |
Marketplace **S**
Liberty House, Ala Moana Shopping Ctr., 1450 Ala Moana Blvd.
(bet. Atkinson Dr. & Piikoi St.), Honolulu, 808-945-8888
Hawaii's answer to Zabar's in NYC, this upscale deli/ grocery in the Liberty House department store showcases award-winning chef Alan Wong's Hawaiian Regional preparations along with the best of the islands' produce, seafood, meats and even chocolate.

Hee Hing **S**   20 | 16 | 15 | $19 |
449 Kapahulu Ave. (opp. Ala Wai golf course), Honolulu,
808-735-5544
■ "Industrial-strength, no-nonsense" Chinese cooking awaits at this Kapahulu spot that's a "favorite" for "yum-yum dim sum"; "slightly rude" service tarnishes its luster for some, but overall this "family favorite" "meets expectations."

HOKU'S **S**   26 | 26 | 25 | $48 |
Kahala Mandarin Oriental Hotel, 5000 Kahala Ave.,
Honolulu, 808-739-8779
■ The name means 'star' in Hawaiian, and surveyors say this "classy" yet "informal" International set in a top- drawer hotel is celestial in every way; "breathtaking views", "delicate, nonrushed" service and "amazing food" via the open kitchen of chef Christopher Vessaire come together for a "first-class" "fine dining" experience; the only quibbles: "costly" tabs and "a little too much noise."

Hong Kong Noodle House **S** ⊅   22 | 8 | 18 | $10 |
Chinese Cultural Plaza, 100 N. Beretania St. (River St.),
Honolulu, 808-536-5409
■ For a "good value" on "oodles of noodles", try this family-run Chinatown Asian that's just the ticket for a "quick, cheap bite"; though not much on looks, its "friendly, helpful staff" "remembers your preferences"; lunch only.

Hy's Steak House **S**   25 | 23 | 23 | $42 |
Waikiki Park Heights Hotel, 2440 Kuhio Ave. (Uluniu Ave.),
Honolulu, 808-922-5555
☑ "Top-of-the-line", dinner-only American steakhouse in Waikiki done up like an "old boys' club", with lots of "dark wood and a fireplace" that nicely complement its "great steaks and chops" and "heavenly bananas Foster"; though prices are on the "expensive" side, fans call it "a solid value."

I Love Country Cafe 🆂 | 18 | 10 | 15 | $11 |
Ala Moana Plaza, 451 Piikoi St. (Kona St.), Honolulu, 808-596-8108
95-1249 Meheula Pkwy. (Lanikuhana Ave.), Mililani, 808-625-5555

I Love Country Cafe Express 🆂
Kahala Mall, 4211 Waialae Ave., Honolulu, 808-735-6965
☑ An "amazing" variety of "healthy choices" awaits (there are a "zillion menu options") at these Eclectic triplets with outposts in Ala Moana, Kahala and Mililani that are known for their "nongreasy plate lunches"; the "very generous servings" arrive in "cafeteria-like" surroundings patronized by a "gym member" crowd.

Indigo | 23 | 22 | 21 | $30 |
1121 Nuuanu Ave. (Hotel St.), Honolulu, 808-521-2900
■ "Always an adventure", this Eurasian "culinary treasure" in Chinatown offers a "unique" mix of "interesting" cuisines – everything from potstickers to pizza – in a "Polynesian atmosphere" complete with an "enchanting garden patio"; though many describe the food as "shockingly good", a very vocal minority derides its "small portions, high cost" formula.

Island Manapua Factory 🆂🚱 | 16 | 7 | 13 | $8 |
Manoa Mktpl., 2752 Woodlawn Dr., Honolulu, 808-988-5441
☑ "Decor doesn't matter" at this "nothing fancy" Manoa Marketplace plate lunch specialist – there's hardly "enough space to dine" anyway – so most recommend it as a "takeout only" venue; still, a fine "variety of *manapua*" and other "cheap, filling" eats make the "long lines understandable."

Jameson's by the Sea 🆂 | 18 | 19 | 18 | $29 |
62-540 Kamehameha Hwy., Haleiwa, 808-637-4336
☑ Worth the "long drive" solely for its "spectacular setting", this Haleiwa seafooder draws diners "by default – what else is there on the North Shore?"; while many allow that the food is "nice, but not memorable", just as many "wish they'd change the menu", but there's absolutely no need to fix the "wonderful sunsets."

Jimbo Restaurant 🆂 | 20 | 12 | 16 | $12 |
1936 S. King St. (McCully St.), Honolulu, 808-947-2211
■ There's a reason for the perpetual "line outside" this "small" McCully Japanese: "authentic", "homemade" noodles that represent some of the "best udon and soba in Hawaii"; "inexpensive" prices also keep it "buzzing all the time", so much so that there's "not enough parking."

John Dominis 🆂 | 20 | 24 | 20 | $45 |
43 Ahui St. (Ala Moana Blvd.), Honolulu, 808-523-0955
☑ Seafarers "love the fish tank" and the "dramatic views" of "Honolulu city lights" at this Continental seafooder off Ala Moana, now in its 20th year; landlubbers, however, decry the "mediocre food", "tarnished" decor and "way too expensive" tabs, though there's consensus that you should "go if someone else is paying."

Kakaako Kitchen   21 | – | 15 | $12

Ward Ctr., 1200 Ala Moana Blvd. (bet. Auahi & Kamakee Sts.),
Honolulu, 808-596-7488
■ "Gourmet plate lunches" grace the menu of this Euro-
Japanese that's "always busy" and thus best for takeout; its
"extremely friendly staff" and "down-to-earth prices" elate
fans, but the jury's still out on their new Ward Centre digs.

Keo's 🅂   23 | 22 | 19 | $26

Ambassador Hotel, 2028 Kuhio Ave. (Kuamoo St.),
Honolulu, 808-951-9355
Ward Ctr., 1200 Ala Moana Blvd. (bet. Auahi St. & Ward Ave.),
Honolulu, 808-596-0020
■ These Thai seafooders are "popular" "celeb magnets",
thanks to "delicious" fare made from "fresh", "high-quality"
ingredients ("just reading the menu makes my mouth
water"); some say the Waikiki outpost "lost its funky decor
and charm" following its move to the Ambassador Hotel, but
at least the move "hasn't dampened its explosive flavors."

Kim Chee II 🅂🖵   19 | 8 | 13 | $11

3569 Waialae Ave. (bet. 11th & 12th Aves.), Honolulu,
808-737-7733
■ The portions at this Kaimuki Korean diner are so
"generous" that there's usually "enough for dinner and
tomorrow's lunch"; and though there's "no atmosphere", no
one seems to mind as the food is "tasty", "fast and cheap."

Kincaid's Fish, Chop &   22 | 20 | 21 | $27
Steak House ◐🅂

Ward Warehouse, 1050 Ala Moana Blvd. (bet. Piikoi St. &
Ward Ave.), Honolulu, 808-591-2005
■ It's "the attention to detail" that "elevates" this Ward
Warehouse surf 'n' turfer above the competition; expect
"great value", "consistently good service" and "ooh-la-la
crème brûlée" at this "solid" place.

Kirin ◐🅂   21 | 13 | 15 | $23

2518 S. Beretania St. (1 block west of University Ave.),
Honolulu, 808-942-1888
■ "Everything tastes great" at this "high-quality" Chinese
near the University, where "inspiring dishes" like the "super
baked crab" and "excellent pepper shrimp" draw huzzahs; a
"comfortable atmosphere" and late hours (till 2 AM) also
keep it hopping with "lots of locals."

Kobe 🅂   21 | 17 | 19 | $30

1841 Ala Moana Blvd. (Kalia Rd.), Honolulu, 808-941-4444
■ It's "showtime" when the knives start flying at this "fun",
"Benihana-esque" teppanyaki spot in Waikiki where you can
"eat and be entertained" by chefs slicing and dicing "great
steak and scallops"; fresh air fanatics fume it "needs better
ventilation", and skinflints fuss about "high prices", but
overall, "you get your money's worth" here.

Kua'Aina Sandwich 🅂⊄ | 22 | 13 | 14 | $10 |
66-214 Kamehameha Hwy. (Opaeula Rd.), Haleiwa,
808-637-6067
Ward Village Shops, 1116 Auahi St. (Kamakee St.),
Honolulu, 808-591-9133
■ The "crowds speak for themselves" at these patty palaces in Haleiwa and near Ala Moana that are "musts for hamburger lovers" ("the best on the planet"), who note that the "shoestring fries are good too"; aficionados "prefer [the original] Haleiwa" outpost over its younger sibling and "hate it when they are out of avocado", a favorite topping.

Kyotaru Hawaii | 19 | 14 | 17 | $16 |
Pioneer Plaza, 900 Fort St. Mall, Honolulu,
808-538-7762 ⊄
Bishop Sq., 1001 Bishop St., Honolulu, 808-528-0150
2154 Kalakaua Ave. (opp. Wyland Gallery), Honolulu,
808-924-3663 🅂
98-1226 Kaahumanu, Waimalu, 808-487-0091 🅂
■ These "steadfast" Japanese "favorites" in Honolulu and Pearl City offer "delicious" sushi and "reliable" takeout; though a few find them somewhat "pricey", others say they're "good for family dining with children" or for "quick lunches"; N.B. lunch only at Pioneer Plaza.

Kyo-Ya 🅂 | 25 | 25 | 23 | $38 |
2057 Kalakaua Ave., Honolulu, 808-947-3911
■ For an "excellent visual" experience, sample this "consummate" Japanese with "great decor" and "superb, beautifully served" fare; true, it's "very pricey", but for "authentic" dining that's among the "classiest on Waikiki", admirers suggest you "splurge on a leisurely lunch."

LA MER 🅂 | 26 | 27 | 26 | $63 |
Halekulani Hotel, 2199 Kalia Rd. (Lewers St.), Honolulu,
808-923-2311
■ "Tops in all categories", this "legendary" Classic French is the "crème de la crème" of Waikiki, with a "fabulous" menu courtesy of chef Yves Garnier, "outstanding service" and a "très elegant" setting in the Halekulani resort; but "bring lots of money" – it just might be "the most expensive restaurant" around – and don't forget to "wear a sportcoat", required for entry.

Legend Seafood 🅂 | 24 | 13 | 15 | $20 |
Chinese Cultural Plaza, 100 N. Beretania St. (Maunakea St.),
Honolulu, 808-532-1868
■ "Authentic", "top-notch" dim sum draws applause at this "busy" Chinatown Cantonese that's a "good place to try unusual fish"; while a few say it "needs better service" and a face-lift in the decor department, most feel the "fabulous" fare more than makes up for these minor flaws.

Little Bit of Saigon, A ⑤   19 | 12 | 16 | $15
1160 Maunakea St., Honolulu, 808-528-3663
■ Among the dozens of Vietnamese pho shops in Chinatown, this trendy noodle eatery stands out thanks to "healthy", "yummy" cuisine served in a "friendly atmosphere"; even though it could stand a "cheerier look", it's still a "great place to go before the Hawaii Theater."

L'Uraku ⑤   24 | 23 | 22 | $33
Uraku Tower, 1341 Kapiolani Blvd. (Piikoi St.), Honolulu, 808-955-0552
■ "Unique", "whimsical decor" (" beautiful hand-painted umbrellas") plays off chef Hiroshi Fukui's "bright flavors" at this "innovative" Euro-Japanese near Ala Moana whose ratings have risen across the board since our last *Survey;* boosters tout the "light, satisfying dishes", especially the $15, four-course weekend lunch menu that's light on the wallet at this otherwise "pricey" place.

Maple Garden ⑤   21 | 14 | 17 | $18
909 Isenberg St. (King St.), Honolulu, 808-941-6641
■ "Longevity says it all" about this 25-year-old Chinese "neighborhood" spot just 10 minutes from Waikiki; "excellent" "spicy" dishes (including "the best moo shu pork") enliven the "unpretentious" but "comfortable" room where "the John Young artwork is a feast for the eyes."

Mariposa ⑤   20 | 24 | 20 | $27
Neiman Marcus, 1450 Ala Moana Blvd. (opp. Ala Moana Park), Honolulu, 808-951-3420
◪ "Neiman Marcus meets the tropics" at this "beautiful, beautiful, beautiful" Pacific Rim–Southwesterner located on the department store's third floor in Ala Moana; though many praise the "amazing view" and "genius" chef Doug Lum (and his "fresh-from-the-oven" lunchtime popovers), others find the enterprise marred by "slow service" and sniff it's "overpriced, like the store."

Matteo's ⑤   20 | 19 | 20 | $35
Marine Surf Hotel, 364 Seaside Ave. (Kuhio Ave.), Honolulu, 808-922-5551
◪ If "old-time dining" in a "dimly lit" room with big "leather booths" and "waiters in tuxedos" appeals, try this "fantastic" Waikiki Italian veteran (since 1972) that's renowned for its "excellent wine list"; though modernists moan that this "boring", "faded" place "needs to be freshened up", loyalists insist it can't be beat for "very romantic" "special occasions."

Maui Tacos ⑤   18 | 11 | 14 | $11
Kailua Village, 539 Kailua Rd., Kailua, 808-261-4155
Mililani Center, 95-221 Ripapa Dr. (near Schofield Barracks), Mililani, 808-623-9405
See review in Maui Directory.

Mediterraneo ⇥   20 | 16 | 19 | $24
1279 S. King St. (bet. Keeaumoku & Piikoi Sts.), Honolulu,
808-593-1466

■ This "little" "hole-in-the-wall" near Ala Moana features "heavenly" Italian fare courtesy of an "entertaining" chef who "sings" and "cooks from the heart" (he "learned his mama's recipes" well); in short, expect "great pasta" made with "fresh ingredients" served in a "cozy" "bistro setting."

Mekong Thai S   25 | 16 | 19 | $20
1295 S. Beretania St. (Keeaumoku & Piikoi Sts.), Honolulu,
808-591-8842

Mekong Thai II S
1726 S. King St. (McCully St.), Honolulu, 808-941-6184

◪ You "can't go wrong" at these "dependable" Thai siblings that are "as good as Keo's" but offer "lower prices"; habitués say they're just the ticket for everything from takeout to "special group dinners" and particularly recommend the "excellent spring rolls", spicy eggplant and the ominously named Evil Jungle curry.

Michel's S   23 | 25 | 23 | $52
Colony Surf Hotel, 2895 Kalakaua Ave., Honolulu, 808-923-6552

◪ For "high elegance at the ocean's edge", try this dinner-only Continental–New French at the foot of Diamond Head that offers "romantic sunsets to enhance your dining pleasure"; though around since 1960, many applaud its "nice remodel job"; foes "aren't sure about this latest transition" but are convinced it's "terribly expensive."

Mini Garden ●S⇥   19 | 6 | 10 | $10
50 N. Hotel St., Honolulu, 808-538-1273

■ "Cheap" yet "excellent" eats emerge from the kitchen of this "small" Chinatown noodle shop specializing in "Hong Kong–style" fare; its "bad location" does offer an "entertaining view of street life", but for the faint of heart there's always takeout.

Mocha Java Cafe S   18 | 14 | 15 | $11
Ward Ctr., 1200 Ala Moana Blvd. (bet. Piikoi St. & Ward Ave.),
Honolulu, 808-591-9023

■ Amid bustling Ward Centre lies this "health food lover's abode", a "friendly" American-Vegetarian coffee shop that delivers "quick" and "yummy" eats accompanied by "excellent" coffee; it's the perfect spot "to get away from the crowds" or for a "nice break from shopping."

Murphy's Bar & Grill   17 | 17 | 18 | $18
2 Merchant St. (Nuuanu St.), Honolulu, 808-531-0422

■ Maybe "as close to a real pub" as you will find in Hawaii, this Downtown watering hole serves "tasty" black and tans and "homestyle" American fare, along the lines of "hearty" burgers and seafood; still, regulars say "food is not the main attraction" here, but rather the "friendly" "Irish mood."

Naupaka Terrace ☒

22 | 22 | 21 | $32

*JW Marriott Ihilani Resort & Spa, 92-1001 Olani St.,
Kapolei, 808-679-0079*

☑ "Excellent", "interesting" cuisine, a "superb" Sunday brunch, a "beautiful" indoor/outdoor setting and "attentive", "knowledgeable" service make it worth the "long drive" to this "remote" West Oahu Japanese seafooder; penny-pinchers protest the "expensive" tabs, however.

Nick's Fishmarket ☒

22 | 19 | 22 | $40

*Waikiki Gateway Hotel, 2070 Kalakaua Ave. (Olohana St.),
Honolulu, 808-955-6333*

☑ "Hats off to the chef" at this "consistently excellent" Waikiki Italian seafooder where an "outstanding" staff and occasional live music embellish the "romantic" atmosphere, but cynics nix the "dark", "stale" ambiance and "overpriced" food; still, most find it a "pleasant surprise given the name."

Ninniku-Ya Garlic Restaurant ☒

20 | 18 | 19 | $31

3196 Waialae Ave. (bet. 3rd & 4th Aves.), Honolulu, 808-735-0784

☑ "You gotta love garlic" – and beef – to appreciate this "superior" Kaimuki Eurasian where the eponymous herb graces everything on the menu (even ice cream) and arrives in "generous" portions served by a "charming" staff; N.B., since our last *Survey,* management reports that the ventilation system has been improved.

Olive Tree Cafe ☒⊄

23 | 12 | 16 | $14

4614 Kilauea Ave. (Pahoa St.), Honolulu, 808-737-0303

■ The menu at this "no-frills" Kahala "neighborhood" BYO cafe offers "all the best Greek dishes", "consistently" prepared with "high-quality", "fresh" ingredients; the tiny outdoor dining area is "always packed" (probably because everything is so "well-priced") , but for those who "don't like eating in a parking lot", "takeout is the way to go."

OnJin's Cafe

– | – | – | M

401 Kamakee St. (Kapiolani Blvd.), Honolulu, 808-589-1666

Former chef/owner of the Hanatei Bistro, OnJin Kim is now back in the kitchen whipping up her creative, upscale dishes on the site of the former Meeting Place Cafe near Ala Moana; look for Asian plate lunches by day and French bistro style preparations at night.

Ono Hawaiian Foods ⊄

23 | 9 | 16 | $13

726 Kapahulu Ave. (bet. Date & Winam Sts.), Honolulu, 808-737-2275

☑ This "casual" eatery on the fringes of Waikiki "lives up to its name" (it translates as 'delicious') and is "da place" for "authentic", "reliable" Hawaiian grinds and "huge" *laulaus*; the "classic, tasty" fare is so highly thought of that you should brace yourself for "long lines" and "difficult" parking.

ORCHIDS ⑤   25 | 27 | 24 | $43

Halekulani Hotel, 2199 Kalia Rd. (Lewers St.), Honolulu, 808-923-2311

■ Located in a "beautiful", "romantic" Waikiki oceanfront setting, this American seafooder is an "oasis" where "five-star" dishes are served by an "impeccable" staff; whether you go for a "delightful" lunch, "lovely" sunset dinner or the "superior" Sunday brunch, diners agree this exercise in "classic hedonism" might be "pricey" but is still a "wonderful splurge."

Outback Steakhouse ⑤   19 | 17 | 18 | $24

1765 Ala Moana Blvd. (Hobron Ln.), Honolulu, 808-951-6274

☑ Loyalists laud the "abundant" servings of "tasty" grub at this "informal" Australian-themed steakhouse franchise that's adjacent to Waikiki's Ilikai Hotel; though dissenters dis the "corporate steaks" as only a "cut above McDonald's", most agree this is "ok chain dining" "for the price" and single out the bloomin' onion appetizer as a "must."

Padovani's Bistro & Wine Bar ⑤   25 | 24 | 23 | $55

Doubletree Alana Hotel, 1956 Ala Moana Blvd. (Kalakaua Ave.), Honolulu, 808-946-3456

☑ "First-class" chef Philippe Padovani (La Mer, Lanai's Ihilani) has created a "bright new star" in Waikiki – a wine bar offering a selection of 48 vintages by the glass abetted by a "superb" Hawaiian bistro menu; "impressive" decor (though there's "no view") adds to the "quality" experience, and most say the "expensive" prices are "worth every penny"; N.B. a mandatory tipping policy has been scratched.

Paesano ⑤   22 | 18 | 20 | $23

2752 Woodlawn Dr., Honolulu, 808-988-5923

☑ If you crave "wonderful home cooking" that's "not fancy" in a "pleasant" neighborhood setting, check out this Manoa Italian "staple" where "even the small portions are generous"; "simple" decor and "gracious" service make this "charming" (though sometimes "crowded") eatery a "great bargain."

Palomino Euro Bistro ⑤   22 | 25 | 21 | $30

Harbor Sq., 66 Queen St. (bet. Bethel & Nimitz Sts.), Honolulu, 808-528-2400

■ "Stunning" decor and a "happening", "lively" atmosphere draw "scenesters" to this "trendy" Downtown American-Mediterranean where the "creative" cooking comes at "reasonable" prices; the only drawback at this "oh so cosmopolitan" spot seems to be the service, which some say "depends on who you are or appear to be."

Panda Cuisine ◖Ⓢ   20   14   14 $16
641 Keeaumoku St. (Makaloa), Honolulu, 808-947-1688
☑ This Chinese seafooder near Ala Moana offers "quick"
dim sum, "excellent" kung pau chicken and "wonderful"
seven-course dinners as well as some of the "best" takeout
around; though it can be "noisy" and "crowded" and the
staff "could improve" in the "attitude" department, it's
"cheap" enough for most to overlook these lapses.

Parc Cafe Ⓢ   22   19   21 $26
Waikiki Parc Hotel, 2233 Helumoa Rd. (Kalia Rd.),
Honolulu, 808-931-6643
■ Even picky eaters rave about the "extensive" buffets
served daily at this "favorite" Waikiki Asian-Hawaiian that's
just the ticket "when entertaining friends"; P.S. the "salads
are so great you may never make it to the entree."

Patisserie, The Ⓢ   19   11   14 $13
Kahala Mall, 4211 Waialae Ave. (next to Star Supermarket),
Honolulu, 808-735-4402
■ "You'll never leave hungry" after sampling some of
the "outstanding" German fare at this bakery/deli with
"a European feeling" in the Kahala Mall; though some
disparage the "not friendly" staff, most compare it to
"eating in the kitchen at home" – you "can't go wrong" here.

Pineapple Room Ⓢ   –   –   –   E
Liberty House, Ala Moana Shopping Ctr., 1450 Ala Moana Blvd.
(Atkinson Dr.), Honolulu, 808-945-8881
The remarkable Hawaiian Regional cuisine of chef Alan
Wong is now available for breakfast, lunch and dinner in an
airy, tropical room complete with an exhibition kitchen on
the third floor of a department store at Ala Moana Shopping
Center; nothing here is traditional, from the Chinese braised
roast duck for breakfast to the ahi meat loaf for lunch.

Plumeria Beach Cafe Ⓢ   22   24   21 $31
Kahala Mandarin Oriental Hotel, 5000 Kahala Ave.,
Honolulu, 808-739-8760
☑ Nestled in a "spectacular" beachfront setting in the
Kahala Mandarin Hotel, this "casual" Eclectic offers
"high-quality" buffets with "good variety"; "friendly"
service and "beautiful" views make it a "relaxing" albeit
"expensive" island getaway for "both guests and locals."

Prince Court Restaurant Ⓢ   23   22   22 $36
Hawaii Prince Hotel Waikiki, 100 Holomoana St.
(Ala Moana Blvd.), Honolulu, 808-944-4494
■ This Waikiki American-Japanese overlooking Ala Wai
Yacht Harbor remains a "favorite" (particularly for special
occasions or "expense-account" meals), even after the
departure of popular chef Gary Strehl; credit "impressive"
buffets, "outstanding" desserts and "delicious" Sunday
brunches for making this a "great dining experience."

Pyramids, The 🅂   21 | 18 | 19 | $21
758 Kapahulu Ave., Honolulu, 808-737-2900
■ Belly dancers in the evening and "authentic" cooking "transport you to another world" at this Kapahulu Avenue Middle Eastern; the "not-to-be-missed" lunch buffet is "reasonable" and the "intimate" setting feels like you're "eating in someone's home."

Quintero's Cuisine 🅂   19 | 9 | 14 | $16
1102 Piikoi St. (Young St.), Honolulu, 808-593-1561
◪ Proponents praise the "fantastic" kitchen at this Mexican BYO near Ala Moana, while admitting that this "hole-in-the-wall" "looks run-down", "service needs to improve" and –"ay carumba! – parking is a problem"; still, wallet-watchers say the "low" prices "overshadow" these shortcomings.

Restaurant Suntory 🅂   23 | 20 | 20 | $39
Royal Hawaiian Shopping Ctr., 2233 Kalakaua Ave. (Royal Hawaiian Ave.), Honolulu, 808-922-5511
◪ Ok, it might be "way overpriced", but that doesn't deter fans from savoring the "great experience" of this Japanese in the Royal Hawaiian Shopping Center; clock watchers say they "don't feel rushed" while enjoying "excellent" teppanyaki and sushi in the "beautifully decorated" room.

Royal Garden ◗🅂   23 | 21 | 17 | $25
Ala Moana Hotel, 410 Atkinson Dr. (bet. Ala Moana & Kapiolani Blvds.), Honolulu, 808-942-7788
◪ Cantonese seafooder located in the Ala Moana Hotel that wins kudos for its "terrific" Chinese cooking, not to mention some of "the best dim sum in town"; diehards "suffer the noise" and "slow service" in silence while focusing instead on the "convenient late hours."

ROY'S 🅂   26 | 20 | 23 | $42
6600 Kalanianaole Hwy. (Keahole St.), Honolulu, 808-396-7697
■ The "original" Hawaii Kai flagship of the global chain founded by award-winning chef/owner Roy Yamaguchi (the "leader in Pacific Rim cuisine") is "still the best", thanks to always "innovative" cuisine from the "wonderful" open kitchen, a "friendly" staff and the "best" sunset views around; but the "packed-in tables" and "intolerable noise level" in the main dining room make eating in the lounge an option to consider, short of bringing "earplugs."

RUTH'S CHRIS STEAK HOUSE 🅂   26 | 20 | 23 | $42
Restaurant Row, 500 Ala Moana Blvd. (bet. Punchbowl & South Sts.), Honolulu, 808-599-3860
■ Carnivores crow that "you'll leave happy and full" after dining at this "high-energy" Restaurant Row chain chop shop where the "à la carte everything" includes "oh so tender" steaks that are "consistent 100 percent of the time"; a "great wine list" ("three different Turley's – rare for Hawaii") rounds out this impressive, if "pricey", experience.

Ryan's Grill ◐ S
19 18 19 $23
Ward Ctr., 1200 Ala Moana Blvd. (bet. Piikoi St. & Ward Ave.), Honolulu, 808-591-9132

■ "Power lunchers" and the "younger set" are drawn to this Contemporary American by its "tasty", "unpretentious" fare, "well-stocked" bar, "fast", "friendly" service and central location in Ward Centre; though some gripe that the "food is declining", most feel this "happening" meeting place is "still good after all these years."

Salerno S
20 16 18 $23
McCully Shopping Ctr., 1960 Kapiolani Blvd., 2nd fl. (McCully St.), Honolulu, 808-942-5273

■ "Italian for those who appreciate good Italian", this McCully spot dishes out "hardy" fare (including one of "best classic Caesars" around) in "large" portions; though this "cozy", quiet "getaway" might be in a not-too-scenic spot (a "great view of traffic"), most turn a blind eye and focus instead on the "reasonable" prices.

Sam Choy's Breakfast, Lunch & Crab S
20 19 18 $25
580 N. Nimitz Hwy. (opp. Gentry Pacific Design Ctr.), Honolulu, 808-545-7979

☑ "You won't leave hungry" from this "friendly" Hawaiian seafooder located in Iwilei, thanks to its "enormous" servings of "homestyle" cooking; "*ono*" fried *poke*, "succulent king crab" that "falls off your plate" and the "best brewpub beer in Oahu" reward patience at this "always crowded" local "favorite", where waits can be "long" and service "slow."

Sam Choy's Diamond Head S
23 20 22 $36
Hee Hing Plaza, 449 Kapahulu Ave. (opp. Ala Wai Golf Course), Honolulu, 808-732-8645

☑ "Sit at the chef's bar" and watch the kitchen prepare "obscenely huge portions" of "rich" but "interesting" Hawaiian Regional combinations at this Waikiki branch of local boy Sam Choy's dining empire; while a few wonder "what's all the hype about?", there's no doubt that the "outstanding Sunday brunch" is a safe bet; N.B. don't miss the new, aloha-style tapas menu.

Sarento's Top of the I S
21 24 22 $40
Ilikai Hotel, 1777 Ala Moana Blvd., Honolulu, 808-955-5559

■ "Breathtaking" 360-degree views of Diamond Head, Waikiki and Honolulu's city lights provide the "stunning" backdrop at this "true dining experience" atop the Ilikai Hotel; fans say this "romantic" Italian is "outstanding in every detail", from its "excellent food and wine list" to service that "makes you feel like royalty" – and those on a budget say the early-bird special is a "winner."

Scoozee's S   18 | 16 | 18 | $18
Ward Ctr., 1200 Ala Moana Blvd. (Auahi St.), Honolulu, 808-597-1777

◪ "The price is right" (nothing over $10 on the menu) at this "convenient" Ward Centre Italian where "generous servings" of "fresh", "reliable" food make it a "good place" for lunch or a "quick family bite"; nitpickers are "not impressed" by the "no-atmosphere" atmosphere and "can't see what the appeal is."

Shogun S   20 | 18 | 19 | $26
Pacific Beach Hotel, 2490 Kalakaua Ave. (Lilioukalani Ave.), Honolulu, 808-921-6113

◪ This Waikiki hotel Japanese is the "local's choice" for "excellent" buffets (especially on holidays), "yummy" sushi and teppanyaki "without the annoying theater"; some find the food "ok" though "not distinguished", but tightwads tout the "huge early-bird special."

Shore Bird Beach Broiler S   16 | 18 | 15 | $21
Outrigger Reef Hotel, 2169 Kalia Rd. (bet. Beachwalk & Lewers Sts.), Honolulu, 808-922-2887

■ You "can't complain about the cooking" at this BBQ surf 'n' turfer fronting Waikiki Beach since "you do it yourself"; although this might be "great for tourists", the "cook-your-own-food" concept doesn't sit well with many locals who wonder "why go out to dinner?"; N.B. there is kitchen (and waiter) service available downstairs.

Singha Thai S   23 | 21 | 20 | $30
Canterbury Pl., 1910 Ala Moana Blvd. (Ena Rd.), Honolulu, 808-941-2898

■ For "exceptionally good", "innovative" Thai cooking with "high-quality ingredients", check out this "elegant" Waikiki eatery which offers "first-class" service as well as nightly entertainment by the Royal Thai Dancers ("a great draw"); though a few say the portions are "too small for the price", far more feel it offers "everything you want when going out."

Strawberry Connection   23 | 9 | 15 | $16
Deli-Grill S
1931 Kahai St. (bet. Mokauea St. & Puuhale Rd.), Honolulu, 808-842-0278

■ The "farm-fresh" International deli fare offered in this converted warehouse is a "best-kept secret" in the "offbeat" Sand Island industrial area; fans connect with the "delicious dishes" and "friendly" service, and though some items are "pricey" and "parking is a problem", the "home-cooked" tastes are still "worth the trip."

Oahu   F D S C

Sunset Grill S   21 | 20 | 20 | $27
Restaurant Row, 500 Ala Moana Blvd. (bet. Punchbowl & South Sts.), Honolulu, 808-521-4409

■ This "consistently good" New American on Restaurant Row is a popular stop for a "yummy" bite (including some "fantastic" fin fare) matched with an "awesome wine list"; the "noisy but fun" environment is fine for both "business" and "family" dining, and crayons are provided to "design your own place setting."

Surf Room S   20 | 24 | 22 | $38
Royal Hawaiian Hotel, 2259 Kalakaua Ave. (Royal Hawaiian Ave.), Honolulu, 808-931-7194

■ "Mom and dad's honeymoon hotel" is the setting for this "old favorite" in Waikiki, a "beautiful", open-air beachfront American-Continental where "gracious hosts" ensure that everyone enjoys themselves; foodwise, it's recommended for the "excellent" Friday lunch buffet (try the bread pudding) and "outstanding" Sunday brunch.

Swiss Inn S   24 | 18 | 24 | $27
Niu Valley Shopping Ctr., 5730 Kalanianaole Hwy. (E. Halemaumau St.), Honolulu, 808-377-5447

■ All are "made to feel welcome" at this Niu Valley Continental-Swiss "institution" where the "incomparable gourmet" cooking is enhanced by "excellent aloha service" from hosts Martin and Jeanie Wyss; the "homey" dining room is often "crowded", especially when the "great Sunday brunch" is in swing.

Tai-Pan on the Boulevard S   23 | 21 | 22 | $34
1680 Kapiolani Blvd. (bet. Atkinson Dr. & Kaheka St.), Honolulu, 808-943-1888

■ Possibly "Honolulu's best-kept secret", this "hidden" spot near Ala Moana features an "extensive" menu of "nouveau" Eclectic eats that "deserve more attention"; following through with "beautiful decor" and "warm hospitality", it's a "real winner."

Tanaka of Tokyo S   22 | 20 | 23 | $31
Ilikai Hotel, 1777 Ala Moana Blvd. (Hobron Ln.), Honolulu, 808-945-3443
King's Village, 131 Kaiulani Ave., 3rd fl. (Koa Ave.), Honolulu, 808-922-4233
Waikiki Shopping Plaza, 2250 Kalakaua Ave., 4th fl. (Seaside Ave.), Honolulu, 808-922-4702

■ The knifes flash, the food flies and "the kids love it" at this Waikiki Japanese steakhouse trio where the "entertaining" chefs pride themselves on "fresh, tasty" "teppanyaki that's better than Benihana's"; the "great service" and "fun atmosphere" appeal to "tourists" and natives alike.

www.zagat.com   75

3660 ON THE RISE 🅂 25 | 20 | 22 | $39
3660 Waialae Ave. (Wilhelmina Rise), Honolulu, 808-737-1177
◼ "Nouvelle Pacific Rim cuisine at its best" wins raves for this "cutting-edge" Kaimuki entry led by "innovative", "outstanding" chef Russell Siu; after a recent redo there are fewer tables and "a more relaxed", "personable" ambiance, and partisans predict this "consistent" "favorite" could "reach the top."

Tony Roma's 🅂 19 | 14 | 17 | $22
1972 Kalakaua Ave. (Ala Moana Blvd.), Honolulu, 808-942-2121
4230 Waialae Ave., Honolulu, 808-735-9595
98-150 Kaonohi St. (opp. Pearlridge Shopping Ctr.), Aiea, 808-487-9911
◪ "Pig out" on "large portions" of "finger-lickin' good" chow at this American BBQ chain where the style might be "basic" yet there's always "good all-around" value; since they're eternally "crowded", the claustrophobic suggest takeout.

Trattoria 🅂 20 | 18 | 19 | $30
Edgewater Hotel, 2168 Kalia Rd. (Beach Walk St.), Honolulu, 808-923-8415
◪ A Waikiki veteran, this Northern Italian is favored for its "delicious" fare ("best Caesar salad anywhere") and a "beautiful" frescoed interior that makes the room "feel like Italy"; even though a few critics carp it's "a little pricey" and "too dark", the budget-minded tout the "cheap" early bird.

Verbano Italiano Ristorante 🅂 20 | 14 | 18 | $21
1451 S. King St. (bet. Kaheka & Keeaumoku Sts.), Honolulu, 808-941-9168
3571 Waialae Ave. (bet. 11th & 12th Aves.), Honolulu, 808-735-1777
◪ For "simple" Italian fare on a "budget night out", this "casual" couple "can't be beat"; sophisticates sniff they're "nothing special", but both branches offer "fast service" and "fair prices" – just what folks want from a pastaria.

Wailana Coffee House ●🅂 14 | 10 | 17 | $13
1860 Ala Moana Blvd. (Kalia Rd.), Honolulu, 808-955-1764
◪ This "24-hour" Waikiki "institution" is a "lifesaver at 4 AM", serving "decent" "coffee shop fare" including "breakfast at any time"; surveyors either love this "old favorite" and its "dependable" "comfort food" or grumble it's "a last resort" – but all agree it's an "economical" choice.

Wasabi Bistro 🅂 20 | 19 | 18 | $26
1006 Kapahulu Ave. (Kaimuki Ave.), Honolulu, 808-735-2800
◪ An "intimate" spot in Diamond Head where chef Yasuzo Ueda's "quite tasty" neo-Japanese offers an "interesting" alternative to "stereotypical" tastes; the "friendly staff" "bends over backwards", and if penny-pinchers protest "too expensive", those in the know observe it's "cheaper at lunch."

Willows, The 🅂   – | – | – | M

901 Hausten St. (King St.), Honolulu, 808-952-9200
Old-time local favorite that was the site of countless
special-occasion celebrations, now reopened at its old
McCully location; traditionalists will be pleased to know it
continues to serve mouthwatering Hawaiian buffets (as
well as à la carte items) for lunch and dinner at very
reasonable prices in a lush, tropical garden atmosphere.

Won Kee Seafood 🅂   21 | 13 | 14 | $22

Chinese Cultural Plaza, 100 N. Beretania St.
(bet. Maunakea & River Sts.), Honolulu, 808-524-6877
■ Among Chinatown's countless seafooders, this
Cantonese is a standout for its "very fresh" fish and
"Hong Kong–style" cooking, including a "must-have"
crab with black bean sauce; admirers are won over by
the "great food" and "good value."

Yanagi Sushi ◑🅂   23 | 17 | 17 | $29

762 Kapiolani Blvd. (bet. Cooke St. & Ward Ave.),
Honolulu, 808-597-1525
◪ After 20-plus years, this Kakaako Japanese still ranks
among "the best" thanks to its "fresh", "authentic sushi",
"outstanding" udon and shabu-shabu, and "great sake
selection"; foes frown it's "crowded" and "overpriced",
but to enthusiasts the "consistent quality" is "worth every
penny" and, as a bonus, it's "open late."

Yohei Sushi   25 | 16 | 19 | $31

Kokea Business Complex, 1111 Dillingham Blvd. (Kokea St.),
Honolulu, 808-841-3773
◪ Despite an "out-of-the-way" location on the edge of
Kalihi, reservations are strongly recommended for this
"always crowded" Japanese seafooder with "one of the
best sushi bars in town"; signature dishes include soba
and the Yohei bento box at lunch and tempura and broiled
salmon at dinner.

Indexes to Restaurants

Special Features and Appeals

CUISINES*

American (New)

Aaron's Atop the Ala Moana
Brew Moon
California Pizza Kitchen
Cascada
David Paul's Lahaina/M
Haliimaile Gen. Store/M
Henry Clay's Rotisserie/L
Ilima Terrace/K
JJ's Broiler/K
Koa Hse. Grill/H
Kona Inn/H
Lodge at Koele/Dining Rm./L
Pahu i'a/H
Ryan's Grill
Seaside/H
Sunset Grill

American (Traditional)

Brennecke's Bch. Broiler/K
Charley's/M
Cheeseburger in Paradise
Cheeseburger in Paradise/M
Chowder House
Contemporary Museum
Duane's Ono-Char/K
Duke's Canoe Club
Duke's Canoe Club/K
Hanalei Wake-Up/K
Hard Rock Cafe
Hard Rock Cafe/H
Hard Rock Cafe/M
Harrington's/H
Hau Tree Lanai
Hy's Steak Hse.
Joe's B&G/M
Joe's Courtside Cafe/K
Joe's on the Green/K
Kea Lani/M
Kincaid's
Kona Ranch Hse./H
Manago Hotel/H
Maunaloa Room/MO
Mocha Java
Murphy's B&G
Ohia Lodge/MO
Ono Family Rest./K
Orchids
Pacific Grill/M

Palomino
Paniolo Country Inn/H
Pioneer Inn/M
Plantation Hse. of Poipu/K
Prince Court/M
Prince Court Rest.
Surf Room
Teshima/H
Tomkats Grille/K
Tony Roma's
Tony Roma's/M
Wailua Marina/K

Asian

Haliimaile Gen. Store/M
Hamura Saimin Stand/K
Hanohano Room
Hong Kong Noodle Hse.
OnJin's Cafe
Pacific Grill/M
Parc Cafe
Pattaya Asian Cafe/K
Surt's at Volcano Village/H

Bakeries

Kanemitsu Bakery/MO
Patisserie

Bar-B-Q

Dixie Grill BBQ
Shore Bird Bch. Broiler
Tony Roma's
Tony Roma's/M

Cajun/Creole

Bay Club/M
Henry Clay's Rotisserie/L
Roussels/H

Californian

Cafe Haleiwa
Joe's Courtside Cafe/K
Joe's on the Green/K
Orchid Court/H

Chinese

China House
Ciao Mein
Eastern Garden
Fook Yuen

* All restaurants are on the island of Oahu unless otherwise noted
  (H=Big Island of Hawaii; K=Kauai; L=Lanai; M=Maui and
  MO=Molokai).

Golden Dragon
Hanamaulu/K
Hee Hing
Hong Kong Noodle Hse.
Kirin
Legend Seafood
Maple Garden
Mema Thai Chinese/K
Mini Garden
Panda Cuisine
Royal Garden
Won Kee

Coffeehouses
Kalaheo Coffee/K
Mocha Java

Coffee Shops/Diners
Big City Diner - Kaimuki
Blue Ginger Cafe/L
Cafe Laufer
Camp Hse. Grill/K
Coffee Gallery
Eggs 'n Things
Hanalei Wake-Up/K
Ken's Hse. of Pancakes/H
Kokee Lodge/K
Ono Family Rest./K
Tip Top Motel/K
Wailana Coffee

Continental
Aaron's Atop the Ala Moana
Alfred's
Edelweiss/H
Gaylord's at Kilohana/K
John Dominis
Kilauea Lodge/H
Michel's
Quinn's/H
Surf Room
Swiss Inn
Waterfront/M

Delis/Sandwich Shops
Andy's Sandwiches
Ba-Le French Sandwich
Cafe Laufer
Hawaii Reg. Mktpl.
Kokee Lodge/K
Leilani's on the Beach/M
Marco's Grill & Deli/M
Patisserie
Strawberry Connection

Dim Sum
China House
Eastern Garden
Hee Hing
Legend Seafood
Panda Cuisine
Royal Garden

Eclectic/International
Aloha Cafe/H
Buzz's Wharf/M
Cafe Monsarrat
Cafe Pesto/H
Caffe Coco/K
Casa Di Amici/K
Eggbert's/K
Fiascos/H
Gordon Biersch
Green Garden/K
Hoku's
I Love Country Cafe
Kula Lodge/M
Lahaina Coolers/M
Maha's Cafe/H
Molokai Pizza Cafe/MO
Oodles of Noodles/H
Pahu i'a/H
Plumeria Beach Cafe
Seasons/M
Stella Blues/M
Strawberry Connection
Tai-Pan on the Blvd.
Waimea Brewing Co./K
Whalers Brewpub/K

Eurasian
Bali-By-The-Sea
Batik/H
Indigo
Ninniku-Ya Garlic
Roy's
Roy's Kahana B&G/M
Roy's Nicolina/M
Roy's Poipu B&G/K
Roy's Waikoloa B&G/H

Euro-Japanese
Kakaako Kitchen
L'Uraku

French
Beau Soleil
Chez Paul/M
Duc's Bistro
La Bourgogne/H
La Mer

French Bistro
Jacques on the Beach/M
OnJin's Cafe

French (New)
Cafe Miró
Chef Mavro's
Gerard's/M
Michel's
Surt's at Volcano Village/H

German
Patisserie

Greek
Greek Bistro/M
Olive Tree Cafe

Hamburgers
Big City Diner - Kaimuki
Brennecke's Bch. Broiler/K
Bubba Burgers/K
Cheeseburger in Paradise
Cheeseburger in Paradise/M
Duane's Ono-Char/K
Hard Rock Cafe
Hard Rock Cafe/H
Hard Rock Cafe/M
Kua'Aina Sandwich
Murphy's B&G
Tomkats Grille/K

Hawaiian
Ahi's Punaluu
Don's Grill/H
Grace's Drive Inn
Island Manapua
Kona Village Luau/H
Manago Hotel/H
Ocean View Inn/H
Old Lahaina Luau/M
Ono Hawaiian Foods
Sam Sato's/M
Willows

Hawaiian Regional
Alan Wong's
Anuenue Room/M
A Pacific Cafe/K
A Pacific Cafe/M
Bali-By-The-Sea
Bamboo/H
Beach House/K
Brown's Beach Hse./H
Chai's Island Bistro
Chef Mavro's

Coast Grille/H
Diamond Head Grill
Don Ho's
Hawaii Reg. Mktpl.
Huggo's/H
Hula Grill/M
Keei Cafe/H
Kimo's/M
Manele Bay/Hulopo'e Court/L
Merriman's/H
Milagros Food Co./M
pacific'O/M
Padovani's Bistro
Palm Cafe/H
Parc Cafe
Pineapple Room
Plantation House/M
Prince Court/M
Roy's Kahana B&G/M
Sam Choy's Breakfast
Sam Choy's Diamond Head
Sam Choy's Kahului/M
Sam Choy's Lahaina/M
Sansei Seafood/M
Seawatch/M
Tidepools/K

Health Food
I Love Country Cafe
Pauwela Cafe/M
Postcards Cafe/K

Indonesian
Sibu Cafe/H

Italian
(N=Northern; S=Southern;
N&S=Includes both)
Angelo Pietro (N&S)
Assaggio (N&S)
Auntie Pasto's (N&S)
Baci Bistro (N&S)
Cafe Che Pasta (N&S)
Cafe Portofino/K (N)
Cafe Sistina (N)
Carelli's on the Beach/M (N&S)
Casanova/M (N&S)
Ciao Mein (N)
Donatoni's/H (N)
Donato's (N&S)
Dondero's/K (N&S)
Ferraro's at Seaside/M (N&S)
Harpo's Pizza (N&S)
La Cascata/K (N&S)
Longhi's/M (N&S)
Marco's Grill & Deli/M (N&S)

Matteo's (N&S)
Mediterraneo (N&S)
Nick's Fishmarket (N&S)
Paesano (N)
Pescatore/H (N&S)
Piatti/K (N&S)
Pomodoro/K (N&S)
Salerno (N&S)
Sarento's Top of the I (N&S)
Scoozee's (N)
Trattoria (N)
Verbano (N&S)

Japanese
Akasaka
Akasaka Marina
Angelo Pietro
Benihana
California Bch. Rock n' Sushi
Genki Sushi
Hakone
Hakone/H
Hakone/M
Hanamaulu/K
Jimbo
Kobe
Kobe/M
Kyotaru Hawaii
Kyo-Ya
L'Uraku
Naupaka Terrace
Ninon/H
Prince Court Rest.
Rest. Kintaro/K
Rest. Suntory
Sansei Seafood/M
Shogun
Tanaka of Tokyo
Teshima/H
Tip Top Motel/K
Tokyo Tei/M
Wasabi Bistro
Yanagi Sushi
Yohei Sushi

Korean
Kim Chee II

Luau
Feast at Lele/M
Kona Village Luau/H
Old Lahaina Luau/M

Mediterranean
Acqua
Azul
Beau Soleil

Cafe Portofino/K
Edward's at Kanaloa/H
Longhi's/M
Manele Bay/Ihilani/L
Palm Court/M
Palomino
Plantation House/M

Mexican
Azteca
Cafe Haleiwa
Compadres
Compadres/M
El Burrito
Maui Tacos
Maui Tacos/H
Maui Tacos/M
Milagros Food Co./M
Polli's/M
Quintero's Cuisine
Reuben's/H
Roadrunner Bakery/K
Tres Hombres/H

Middle Eastern
Pyramids

Noodle Shops
Hong Kong Noodle Hse.
Mini Garden
Oodles of Noodles/H

Pacific Rim
Acqua
A Pacific Cafe
A Pacific Cafe/M
Cafe Hanalei/K
Caffe Coco/K
Canoe House/H
Feast at Lele/M
Gaylord's at Kilohana/K
Hotel Hana-Maui/Dining Rm./M
Hualalai Club Grille/H
i'o/M
Kamuela Provision Co./H
Lodge at Koele/Terrace/L
Manele Bay/Hulopo'e Court/L
Mariposa
Roy's
Roy's Nicolina/M
Roy's Poipu B&G/K
Roy's Waikoloa B&G/H
Sam Choy's Kaloko/H
Shells/K
Swan Court/M
Tahiti Nui/K
3660 on the Rise
Zelo's Beach Hse./K

Pizza
Bianelli's Pizza/H
Boston's North End Pizza
Brennecke's Bch. Broiler/K
Brick Oven Pizza/K
Cafe Pesto/H
California Pizza Kitchen
Harpo's Pizza
Molokai Pizza Cafe/MO

Seafood
Ahi's Punaluu
Bay Terrace/H
Brennecke's Bch. Broiler/K
Bubba Gump Shrimp
Bubba Gump Shrimp/M
Bull Shed/K
Chart House/M
Chowder House
Fook Yuen
Hanalei Dolphin/K
Hanohano Room
Hau Tree Lanai
House of Seafood/K
Hula Grill/M
Jameson's by the Sea/H
Jameson's by the Sea/M
JJ's Broiler/K
John Dominis
Kawaihae Harbor Grill/H
Keoki's Paradise/K
Keo's
Kimo's/M
Kincaid's
Legend Seafood
Mama's Fish House/M
Murphy's B&G
Naupaka Terrace
Nick's Fishmarket
Nick's Fishmarket/M
Orchids
Paia Fishmarket/M
Panda Cuisine
Royal Garden
Sam Choy's Breakfast
Sansei Seafood/M
Seawatch/M
Tidepools/K
Village Grill/MO
Wailua Marina/K
Waterfront/M
Won Kee
Yohei Sushi
Zelo's Beach Hse./K

Southern/Soul
Dixie Grill BBQ

Southwestern
Mariposa

Steakhouses
Big Island Steak Hse.
Big Island Steak Hse./H
Bull Shed/K
Buzz's Original Steakhse.
Chart House
Chart House/H
Chart House/M
Hanalei Dolphin/K
Hy's Steak Hse.
Kalaheo Steak Hse./K
Keoki's Paradise/K
Kincaid's
Kobe
Kobe/M
Leilani's on the Beach/M
Makawao Steak Hse./M
Outback Steakhse.
Outback Steakhse./M
Parker Ranch Grill/H
Ruth's Chris
Ruth's Chris/M
Tanaka of Tokyo
Tidepools/K
Village Grill/MO

Swiss
Alfred's
Swiss Inn

Thai
Chiang Mai
Keo's
Mekong Thai
Mema Thai Chinese/K
Royal Siam/H
Saeng's Thai/M
Singha Thai

Vegetarian
(Most Chinese, Indian and
Thai restaurants)
Hanapepe Cafe/K
Mocha Java
Postcards Cafe/K

Vietnamese
A Saigon Cafe/M
Ba-Le French Sandwich
Duc's Bistro
Hale Vietnam
Little Bit of Saigon

LOCATIONS

BIG ISLAND OF HAWAII

Captain Cook
Keei Cafe
Manago Hotel

Hawi
Bamboo

Hilo
Cafe Pesto
Don's Grill
Fiascos
Harrington's
Ken's Hse. of Pancakes
Maui Tacos
Ninon
Pescatore
Reuben's
Royal Siam
Seaside

Honalo
Teshima

Kailua-Kona
Bianelli's Pizza
Chart House
Edward's at Kanaloa
Hard Rock Cafe
Hualalai Club Grille
Huggo's
Jameson's by the Sea
Kona Inn
Kona Ranch Hse.
Kona Village Luau
La Bourgogne
Ocean View Inn
Oodles of Noodles
Pahu i'a
Palm Cafe

Quinn's
Sam Choy's Kaloko
Sibu Cafe
Tres Hombres

Kainaliu
Aloha Cafe

Kamuela/Waimea
Edelweiss
Koa Hse. Grill
Maha's Cafe
Merriman's
Paniolo Country Inn
Parker Ranch Grill

Kawaihae
Cafe Pesto
Kawaihae Harbor Grill
Tres Hombres

Kohala Coast
Batik
Bay Terrace
Big Island Steak Hse.
Brown's Beach Hse.
Canoe House
Coast Grille
Donatoni's
Hakone
Kamuela Provision Co.
Orchid Court
Roussels
Roy's Waikoloa B&G

Volcano
Kilauea Lodge
Surt's at Volcano Village

KAUAI

Anahola
Duane's Ono-Char

Hanalei
Bubba Burgers
Hanalei Dolphin
Hanalei Wake-Up
Postcards Cafe
Tahiti Nui
Zelo's Beach Hse.

Hanamaulu
Hanamaulu

Hanapepe
Green Garden
Hanapepe Cafe

Kalaheo/Lawai
Brick Oven Pizza
Camp Hse. Grill

Kalaheo Coffee
Kalaheo Steak Hse.
Pomodoro

Kapaa
A Pacific Cafe
Bull Shed
Caffe Coco
Eggbert's
Mema Thai Chinese
Ono Family Rest.
Rest. Kintaro

Kilauea
Roadrunner Bakery

Koloa
Piatti

Lihue
Duke's Canoe Club
Gaylord's at Kilohana
Hamura Saimin Stand
JJ's Broiler
Tip Top Motel
Whalers Brewpub

Nawiliwili
Cafe Portofino

Poipu
Beach House
Brennecke's Bch. Broiler
Casa Di Amici
Dondero's
House of Seafood
Ilima Terrace
Joe's Courtside Cafe
Joe's on the Green
Keoki's Paradise
Pattaya Asian Cafe
Plantation Hse. of Poipu
Roy's Poipu B&G
Shells
Tidepools
Tomkats Grille

Princeville
Cafe Hanalei
La Cascata

Wailua
Wailua Marina

Waimea
Kokee Lodge
Waimea Brewing Co.

LANAI

Blue Ginger Cafe
Henry Clay's Rotisserie
Lodge at Koele/Dining Rm.

Lodge at Koele/Terrace
Manele Bay/Hulopo'e Court
Manele Bay/Ihilani

MAUI

Haiku
Pauwela Cafe

Hana
Hotel Hana-Maui/Dining Rm.

Kaanapali
Hula Grill
Leilani's on the Beach
Swan Court

Kahana
Roy's Kahana B&G
Roy's Nicolina

Kahului
Marco's Grill & Deli
Maui Tacos
Sam Choy's Kahului

Kapalua/Napili
Anuenue Room
Bay Club
Jameson's by the Sea
Maui Tacos
Plantation House
Sansei Seafood

Kihei
A Pacific Cafe
Carelli's on the Beach
Greek Bistro
Jacques on the Beach
Maui Tacos
Palm Court
Stella Blues
Tony Roma's

Kuau
Mama's Fish House

Kula/Makawao/ Haliimaile
Casanova
Haliimaile Gen. Store
Kula Lodge
Makawao Steak Hse.
Polli's

Lahaina
A Pacific Cafe
Bubba Gump Shrimp
Chart House
Cheeseburger in Paradise
Chez Paul
Compadres
David Paul's Lahaina
Feast at Lele
Gerard's
Hard Rock Cafe
i'o
Kimo's
Kobe
Lahaina Coolers
Longhi's
Maui Tacos
Old Lahaina Luau
Outback Steakhse.
pacific'O

Pioneer Inn
Ruth's Chris
Sam Choy's Lahaina

Maalaea
Buzz's Wharf
Waterfront

Paia
Charley's
Jacques on the Beach
Milagros Food Co.
Paia Fishmarket

Wailea/Makena
Chart House
Ferraro's at Seaside
Hakone
Joe's B&G
Kea Lani
Nick's Fishmarket
Pacific Grill
Prince Court
Seasons
Seawatch

Wailuku
A Saigon Cafe
Saeng's Thai
Sam Sato's
Tokyo Tei

MOLOKAI

Kaunakakai
Kanemitsu Bakery

Maunaloa
Maunaloa Room
Molokai Pizza Cafe
Ohia Lodge
Village Grill

OAHU: HONOLULU

Aina Haina/Niu Valley
Swiss Inn

Airport/Mapunapuna
Ba-Le French Sandwich
Strawberry Connection

Ala Moana
Aaron's Atop the Ala Moana
Akasaka
Alan Wong's
Alfred's
Angelo Pietro

Auntie Pasto's
Ba-Le French Sandwich
Cafe Sistina
California Bch. Rock n' Sushi
Chiang Mai
China House
Contemporary Museum
El Burrito
Fook Yuen
Grace's Drive Inn
Hard Rock Cafe
Harpo's Pizza
Hawaii Reg. Mktpl.

I Love Country Cafe
John Dominis
Kua'Aina Sandwich
L'Uraku
Maple Garden
Mariposa
Mediterraneo
Mekong Thai
OnJin's Cafe
Panda Cuisine
Quintero's Cuisine
Royal Garden
Salerno
Tai-Pan on the Blvd.
Tony Roma's
Verbano
Willows
Yanagi Sushi

Downtown: Ala Moana Blvd./Ward Ave.
Bubba Gump Shrimp
Chowder House
Dixie Grill BBQ
Jimbo
Pineapple Room

Downtown: Aloha Tower Marketplace
Big Island Steak Hse.
Chai's Island Bistro
Coffee Gallery
Don Ho's
Gordon Biersch

Downtown: Financial
Ba-Le French Sandwich
Cafe Che Pasta
Harpo's Pizza
Kyotaru Hawaii
Murphy's B&G
Palomino

Downtown: Restaurant Row
Ruth's Chris
Sunset Grill

Downtown: Ward Centre
A Pacific Cafe
Ba-Le French Sandwich
Brew Moon
Compadres
Kakaako Kitchen
Keo's
Kincaid's

Mocha Java
Ryan's Grill
Scoozee's

Downtown: West & Chinatown
Ba-Le French Sandwich
Duc's Bistro
Hong Kong Noodle Hse.
Indigo
Legend Seafood
Little Bit of Saigon
Mini Garden
Sam Choy's Breakfast
Won Kee

Hawaii Kai
Akasaka Marina
Assaggio
Ba-Le French Sandwich
Roy's

Kaimuki/Moiliili
Azteca
Beau Soleil
Big City Diner - Kaimuki
Cafe Miró
Chef Mavro's
Eastern Garden
Grace's Drive Inn
Hale Vietnam
Kim Chee II
Ninniku-Ya Garlic
3660 on the Rise
Verbano

Kapahulu
Cafe Monsarrat
Genki Sushi
Harpo's Pizza
Hee Hing
Ono Hawaiian Foods
Pyramids
Wasabi Bistro

Kapalama/Liliha
Ba-Le French Sandwich
Yohei Sushi

Manoa
Andy's Sandwiches
Island Manapua
Kirin
Paesano

Waialae/Kahala
Ba-Le French Sandwich
Boston's North End Pizza
Cafe Laufer

California Pizza Kitchen
Donato's
Hoku's
I Love Country Exp.
Olive Tree Cafe
Patisserie
Plumeria Beach Cafe

Waikiki

Acqua
Bali-By-The-Sea
Benihana
California Pizza Kitchen
Cascada
Chart House
Cheeseburger in Paradise
Ciao Mein
Diamond Head Grill
Duke's Canoe Club
Eastern Garden
Eggs 'n Things
Golden Dragon
Hakone
Hanohano Room
Hau Tree Lanai
Hy's Steak Hse.

Keo's
Kobe
Kyotaru Hawaii
Kyo-Ya
La Mer
Matteo's
Michel's
Nick's Fishmarket
Orchids
Outback Steakhse.
Padovani's Bistro
Parc Cafe
Prince Court Rest.
Rest. Suntory
Sam Choy's Diamond Head
Sarento's Top of the I
Shogun
Shore Bird Bch. Broiler
Singha Thai
Surf Room
Tanaka of Tokyo
Tony Roma's
Trattoria
Wailana Coffee

OAHU: OTHER LOCATIONS

Aiea/Pearlridge
Ba-Le French Sandwich
Boston's North End Pizza
California Pizza Kitchen
Eastern Garden
Grace's Drive Inn
Tony Roma's

Haleiwa
Cafe Haleiwa
Coffee Gallery
Kua'Aina Sandwich

Kailua
Assaggio
Baci Bistro
Boston's North End Pizza
Buzz's Original Steakhse.
Maui Tacos

Kaneohe
Boston's North End Pizza
Chart House

Eastern Garden
Harpo's Pizza

Kapolei
Azul
Boston's North End Pizza
Naupaka Terrace

Mililani
Assaggio
I Love Country Cafe
Maui Tacos

Pearl City
Buzz's Original Steakhse.
Genki Sushi
Harpo's Pizza
Kyotaru Hawaii

Punaluu
Ahi's Punaluu

SPECIAL FEATURES AND APPEALS*

Breakfast

(All hotels and the
following standouts)
Aloha Cafe/H
Big City Diner - Kaimuki
Cafe Haleiwa
Camp Hse. Grill/K
Charley's/M
Chowder House
Don's Grill/H
Eggbert's/K
Eggs 'n Things
Green Garden/K
Joe's on the Green/K
Kanemitsu Bakery/MO
Kona Ranch Hse./H
Legend Seafood
Longhi's/M
Maha's Cafe/H
Manele Bay/Hulopo'e Court/L
Marco's Grill & Deli/M
Milagros Food Co./M
Ono Family Rest./K
Patisserie
Plantation House/M
Plantation Hse. of Poipu/K
Postcards Cafe/K
Roussels/H
Sam Choy's Breakfast
Seawatch/M
Shells/K
Village Grill/MO
Wailana Coffee

Buffet Served

(Check prices, days
and times)
Bay Club/M
Bay Terrace/H
Cafe Hanalei/K
Duke's Canoe Club/K
Eastern Garden
Fook Yuen
Hakone
Hakone/H
Hanohano Room
Hotel Hana-Maui/Din. Rm./M
Ilima Terrace/K
Indigo

John Dominis
Kawaihae Harbor Grill/H
Kea Lani/M
Keoki's Paradise/K
Kimo's/M
Manele Bay/Hulopo'e Court/L
Naupaka Terrace
Orchids
Palm Cafe/H
Palm Court/M
Parc Cafe
Plumeria Beach Cafe
Prince Court Rest.
Shells/K
Shogun
Shore Bird Bch. Broiler
Surf Room
Swan Court/M
Swiss Inn
Teshima/H
Wailua Marina/K
Willows

Business Dining

Acqua
Alan Wong's
Alfred's
A Pacific Cafe
Azul
Bali-By-The-Sea
Bay Club/M
Cascada
Chef Mavro's
David Paul's Lahaina/M
Duc's Bistro
Hakone
Hakone/H
Hakone/M
Hau Tree Lanai
Hoku's
Indigo
La Bourgogne/H
La Mer
Matteo's
Merriman's/H
Michel's
Nick's Fishmarket
Orchids
Outback Steakhse.

---

* All restaurants are on the island of Oahu unless otherwise noted
(H=Big Island of Hawaii; K=Kauai; L=Lanai; M=Maui and
MO=Molokai).

Outback Steakhse./M
Padovani's Bistro
Pahu i'a/H
Palomino
Prince Court Rest.
Roy's
Roy's Kahana B&G/M
Roy's Nicolina/M
Roy's Waikoloa B&G/H
Ruth's Chris
Ruth's Chris/M
Sam Choy's Diamond Head
Sarento's Top of the I
Seasons/M
Tai-Pan on the Blvd.
Tanaka of Tokyo
Tony Roma's
Village Grill/MO

BYO

Ba-Le French Sandwich
Beau Soleil
Boston's North End Pizza
Bubba Burgers/K
Cafe Haleiwa
Caffe Coco/K
Eggs 'n Things
Genki Sushi
Hanapepe Cafe/K
Jimbo
Kakaako Kitchen
Kalaheo Steak Hse./K
Kua'Aina Sandwich
Little Bit of Saigon
Maha's Cafe/H
Maui Tacos/M
Mekong Thai
Olive Tree Cafe
Ono Family Rest./K
Patisserie
Pauwela Cafe/M
Quintero's Cuisine
Strawberry Connection

Caters

(Best of many)
Alfred's
A Pacific Cafe
Bamboo/H
Beau Soleil
Bubba Gump Shrimp/M
Cafe Che Pasta
Chai's Island Bistro
Chiang Mai
Duc's Bistro

Haliimaile Gen. Store/M
Hard Rock Cafe/H
Hawaii Reg. Mktpl.
I Love Country Cafe
Indigo
Jacques on the Beach/M
Joe's B&G/M
Joe's on the Green/K
Keei Cafe/H
Longhi's/M
Maha's Cafe/H
Matteo's
Merriman's/H
Oodles of Noodles/H
pacific'O/M
Piatti/K
Pineapple Room
Plantation House/M
Pomodoro/K
Sam Choy's Breakfast
Sam Choy's Diamond Head
Sansei Seafood/M
Singha Thai
Sunset Grill
Tai-Pan on the Blvd.
Tokyo Tei/M

Dancing/Entertainment

(Check days, times and
performers for entertainment;
D=dancing; best of many)
Aaron's/Ala Moana (D/band)
Acqua (D/Hawaiian/Latin)
Anuenue Room/M (Hawaiian)
A Pacific Cafe (varies)
A Pacific Cafe/M (Hawaiian/jazz)
Bali-By-The-Sea (Hawaiian)
Bamboo/H (Hawaiian)
Batik/H (guitar)
Bay Club/M (piano)
Big City Diner - Kai. (Hawaiian)
Big Island Steak/H (Hawaiian)
Brew Moon (contemporary)
Brown's Beach/H (Hawaiian)
Cafe Hanalei/K (piano bar)
Cafe Portofino/K (harp)
Cafe Sistina (guitar)
Caffe Coco/K (jazz)
Casanova/M (D)
Chai's Island Bistro (Hawaiian)
Charley's/M (duo)
Cheeseburger/Paradise (rock)
Cheeseburger/Paradise/M (rock)
Compadres (Hawaiian)
David Paul's Lahaina/M (jazz)

Diamond Head Grill (vocalist)
Donatoni's/H (violinist)
Donato's (jazz)
Don Ho's (D/Hawaiian)
Duc's Bistro (jazz/piano)
Duke's Canoe Club (Hawaiian)
Duke's Canoe Club/K (Hawaiian)
Feast at Lele/M (luau)
Ferraro's at Seaside/M (duo)
Fiascos/H (D/varies)
Golden Dragon (varies)
Gordon Biersch (varies)
Hanapepe Cafe/K (guitar)
Hanohano Room (D/jazz)
Hard Rock Cafe (rock)
Harrington's/H (Hawaiian)
Hau Tree Lanai (guitar)
Hotel Hana-Maui/M (Hawaiian)
Huggo's/H (D/rock)
Hula Grill/M (D/Hawaiian)
Hy's Steak Hse. (contemporary)
Jameson's/H (Hawaiian)
Joe's/Green/K (Hawaiian)
John Dominis (Hawaiian/jazz)
Kamuela Prov. Co./H (Top 40)
Keoki's Paradise/K (Hawaiian)
Kimo's/M (Hawaiian)
Kincaid's (Hawaiian)
Koa Hse. Grill/H (D/karaoke)
Kona Village Luau/H (luau)
Lahaina Coolers/M (blues/rock)
Leilani's/M (Hawaiian)
Longhi's/M (contemporary rock)
Naupaka Terrace (guitar)
Nick's Fish Mkt. (easy listening)
Ohia Lodge/MO (Hawaiian)
Old Lahaina Luau/M (luau)
pacific'O/M (jazz)
Padovani's Bistro (jazz/rock)
Pahu i'a/H (guitar)
Parker Ranch Grill/H (varies)
Pioneer Inn/M (varies)
Plumeria Bch. Cafe (Hawaiian)
Prince Court/M (Hawaiian)
Pyramids (belly dancing)
Roussels/H (Hawaiian/jazz)
Roy's (Hawaiian/jazz)
Sam Choy's Break. (Hawaiian)
Sansei Seafood/M (karaoke)
Sarento's Top of the I (piano)
Scoozee's (Hawaiian)
Seasons/M (D/Hawaiian)
Singha Thai (dancers)
Surf Room (Hawaiian)
Swan Ct./M (duo/hula dancer)

Tahiti Nui/K (Hawaiian/Tahitian)
Wailana Coffee (guitar/karaoke)
Waimea Brewing/K (Hawaiian)
Whalers Brewpub/K (varies)

Delivers*/Takeout
(Nearly all Asians, coffee
shops, delis, diners and
pasta/pizzerias deliver or do
takeout; here are some
interesting possibilities;
D=delivery, T=takeout; *call
to check range and charges,
if any)
Ahi's Punaluu (T)
Aloha Cafe/H (T)
Angelo Pietro (T)
A Pacific Cafe/M (T)
Assaggio (T)
Bamboo/H (T)
Bay Club/M (T)
Beau Soleil (T)
Big Island Steak Hse./H (T)
Brennecke's Bch. Broiler/K (T)
Buzz's Original Steakhse. (T)
Buzz's Wharf/M (T)
Cafe Haleiwa (T)
Cafe Monsarrat (T)
Cafe Portofino/K (T)
Caffe Coco/K (T)
California Bch. Rock n' Sushi (T)
Cascada (T)
Chowder House (T)
Compadres (T)
Dixie Grill BBQ (T)
Donato's (T)
Don's Grill/H (T)
Duke's Canoe Club/K (T)
Edward's at Kanaloa/H (T)
Eggbert's/K (T)
Gaylord's at Kilohana/K (T)
Greek Bistro/M (T)
Green Garden/K (T)
Hanalei Dolphin/K (T)
Hanamaulu/K (T)
Hanapepe Cafe/K (T)
Hau Tree Lanai (T)
Henry Clay's Rotisserie/L (T)
Hoku's (T)
House of Seafood/K (T)
Hualalai Club Grille/H (T)
Hula Grill/M (T)
Jameson's by the Sea/M (T)
JJ's Broiler/K (T)
Joe's B&G/M (T)

Joe's Courtside Cafe/K (T)
Joe's on the Green/K (T)
Kalaheo Steak Hse./K (T)
Kawaihae Harbor Grill/H (T)
Keei Cafe/H (T)
Ken's Hse. of Pancakes/H (T)
Keoki's Paradise/K (T)
Kilauea Lodge/H (T)
Kimo's/M (T)
Kincaid's (T)
Koa Hse. Grill/H (T)
Kona Inn/H (T)
La Cascata/K (T)
Leilani's on the Beach/M (T)
Little Bit of Saigon (T)
Maha's Cafe/H (T)
Makawao Steak Hse./M (T)
Mariposa (D)
Merriman's/H (T)
Milagros Food Co./M (T)
Murphy's B&G (D,T)
Ohia Lodge/MO (T)
Olive Tree Cafe (T)
Outback Steakhse. (T)
Outback Steakhse./M (T)
Paniolo Country Inn/H (T)
Parker Ranch Grill/H (T)
Pauwela Cafe/M (T)
Pescatore/H (T)
Piatti/K (T)
Pineapple Room (T)
Pioneer Inn/M (T)
Plantation House/M (T)
Plantation Hse. of Poipu/K (T)
Plumeria Beach Cafe (T)
Pomodoro/K (T)
Postcards Cafe/K (T)
Pyramids (T)
Quinn's/H (T)
Quintero's Cuisine (T)
Roadrunner Bakery/K (T)
Roussels/H (T)
Roy's Kahana B&G/M (T)
Roy's Nicolina/M (T)
Ruth's Chris (T)
Ryan's Grill (T)
Sam Choy's Breakfast (T)
Sam Choy's Diamond Head (T)
Sam Choy's Kahului/M (T)
Sam Choy's Kaloko/H (T)
Sam Choy's Lahaina/M (T)
Scoozee's (T)
Seaside/H (T)
Seawatch/M (T)
Stella Blues/M (T)

Sunset Grill (T)
Swiss Inn (T)
3660 on the Rise (T)
Tomkats Grille/K (T)
Tony Roma's (D,T)
Verbano (D,T)
Waimea Brewing Co./K (T)
Waterfront/M (T)
Whalers Brewpub/K (T)
Zelo's Beach Hse./K (T)

Dessert/Ice Cream

Aloha Cafe/H
Big City Diner - Kaimuki
Cafe Laufer
Caffe Coco/K
Charley's/M
Coffee Gallery
Contemporary Museum
David Paul's Lahaina/M
Haliimaile Gen. Store/M
Hanapepe Cafe/K
Huggo's/H
Joe's B&G/M
Ken's Hse. of Pancakes/H
Lahaina Coolers/M
Lodge at Koele/Dining Rm./L
Longhi's/M
Maha's Cafe/H
Manele Bay/Ihilani/L
Merriman's/H
Michel's
Padovani's Bistro
Postcards Cafe/K
Prince Court/M
Sarento's Top of the I
Tip Top Motel/K

Dining Alone

(Other than hotels, coffee
shops, sushi bars and places
with counter service)
Alfred's
Angelo Pietro
Assaggio
Auntie Pasto's
Baci Bistro
Big Island Steak Hse.
Bull Shed/K
Buzz's Original Steakhse.
Cafe Pesto/H
Cafe Portofino/K
California Pizza Kitchen
Chart House
China House

Chowder House
Dixie Grill BBQ
Don's Grill/H
Eastern Garden
Edelweiss/H
Hale Vietnam
Hamura Saimin Stand/K
Hanalei Dolphin/K
Hee Hing
Huggo's/H
I Love Country Cafe
Jameson's by the Sea/H
Kakaako Kitchen
Kawaihae Harbor Grill/H
Kokee Lodge/K
Kona Ranch Hse./H
Maha's Cafe/H
Marco's Grill & Deli/M
Mema Thai Chinese/K
Murphy's B&G
OnJin's Cafe
Outback Steakhse./M
Paesano
Palomino
Panda Cuisine
Pattaya Asian Cafe/K
Roussels/H
Ruth's Chris
Ruth's Chris/M
Sibu Cafe/H
Swiss Inn
Tony Roma's
Village Grill/MO

Early-Bird Menus
(Call to check prices,
days and times)
Aaron's Atop the Ala Moana
Acqua
A Pacific Cafe
Big Island Steak Hse.
Big Island Steak Hse./H
Brennecke's Bch. Broiler/K
Cafe Haleiwa
Cafe Portofino/K
Cafe Sistina
Eggbert's/K
Keoki's Paradise/K
Kincaid's
Kobe
Kobe/M
Kyotaru Hawaii
Nick's Fishmarket
Plantation Hse. of Poipu/K
Roussels/H

Sam Choy's Breakfast
Sam Choy's Lahaina/M
Shore Bird Bch. Broiler
Trattoria
Zelo's Beach Hse./K

Late-Supper Menus
(Call to check prices,
days and times)
Aaron's Atop the Ala Moana
Big City Diner - Kaimuki
Brew Moon
Chart House
Dixie Grill BBQ
Don Ho's
Ken's Hse. of Pancakes/H
Keoki's Paradise/K
Lahaina Coolers/M
Matteo's
Orchids
Palomino
Panda Cuisine
Quinn's/H
Quintero's Cuisine
Ryan's Grill
Sam Choy's Breakfast
Singha Thai
Tai-Pan on the Blvd.

Fireplaces
Edelweiss/H
Henry Clay's Rotisserie/L
Hotel Hana-Maui/Dining Rm./M
Kilauea Lodge/H
Koa Hse. Grill/H
Kokee Lodge/K
Kula Lodge/M
Lodge at Koele/Dining Rm./L
Makawao Steak Hse./M
Manele Bay/Hulopo'e Court/L
Parker Ranch Grill/H
Plantation House/M

Game in Season
Henry Clay's Rotisserie/L
Kilauea Lodge/H
Lodge at Koele/Terrace/L
Makawao Steak Hse./M
Manele Bay/Hulopo'e Court/L
Plumeria Beach Cafe
Prince Court Rest.

Health/Spa Menus

(Most places cook to order to meet any dietary request; call in advance to check; almost all Chinese, Indian and other ethnics have health-conscious meals, as do the following)

Cafe Sistina
Caffe Coco/K
I Love Country Cafe
Joe's Courtside Cafe/K
Manele Bay/Ihilani/L
Mocha Java
Naupaka Terrace
Orchids
Postcards Cafe/K

Historic Interest

(Year opened; *building)

1852	Maha's Cafe/H*
1915	Tip Top Motel/K
1917	Manago Hotel/H
1917	Orchids*
1919	Cafe Pesto/H*
1925	Hanamaulu/K
1925	Surf Room*
1927	Henry Clay's Rotisserie/L*
1928	Makawao Steak Hse./M*
1933	Piatti/K*
1933	Sam Sato's/M
1935	Gaylord's at Kilohana/K*
1935	Ocean View Inn/H
1937	Tokyo Tei/M
1938	David Paul's Lahaina/M*
1942	Teshima/H
1946	Hotel Hana-Maui/Din./M
1947	Seaside/H
1948	Green Garden/K
1950	Kokee Lodge/K
1955	Golden Dragon
1958	Kyo-Ya
1960	Michel's
1962	Buzz's Original Steakhse.
1962	Ono Hawaiian Foods
1963	Hee Hing
1964	Buzz's Wharf/M
1964	Hau Tree Lanai
1964	Pioneer Inn/M
1965	Batik/H
1965	Tahiti Nui/K
1967	JJ's Broiler/K
1968	Chez Paul/M
1968	Nick's Fishmarket
1968	Wailua Marina/K

Hotel Dining

Ala Moana Hotel
  Aaron's Atop the Ala Moana
  Royal Garden
Ambassador Hotel
  Keo's
Best Western Pioneer Inn
  Pioneer Inn/M
Colony Surf Hotel
  Michel's
Doubletree Alana Hotel
  Padovani's Bistro
Edgewater Hotel
  Trattoria
Four Seasons Hualalai
  Hualalai Club Grille/H
  Pahu i'a/H
Four Seasons Resort
  Ferraro's at Seaside/M
  Pacific Grill/M
  Seasons/M
Halekulani Hotel
  La Mer
  Orchids
Hapuna Beach Prince
  Coast Grille/H
  Hakone/H
Hawaii Prince
  Hakone
  Prince Court Rest.
Hawaiian Regent Hotel
  Acqua
Hilton Hawaiian Village
  Bali-By-The-Sea
  Benihana
  Golden Dragon
Hilton Waikoloa Village
  Donatoni's/H
  Kamuela Provision Co./H
Hotel Hana-Maui
  Hotel Hana-Maui/Dining
  Rm./M
Hotel Lanai
  Henry Clay's Rotisserie/L
Hyatt Regency Kauai
  Dondero's/K
  Ilima Terrace/K
  Tidepools/K
Hyatt Regency Maui
  Swan Court/M
Hyatt Regency Waikiki
  Ciao Mein
Ilikai Hotel
  Sarento's Top of the I
  Tanaka of Tokyo

JW Marriott Ihilani Resort
  Azul
  Naupaka Terrace
Kahala Mandarin
  Hoku's
  Plumeria Beach Cafe
Kaluakoi Hotel & Golf Club
  Ohia Lodge/MO
Kapalua Bay Hotel & Villas
  Bay Club/M
Kauai Lagoons Resort
  Whalers Brewpub/K
Kauai Marriott
  Duke's Canoe Club/K
Kea Lani Hotel Suites & Villas
  Kea Lani/M
  Nick's Fishmarket/M
Kiahuna Plantation
  Piatti/K
Kona Village Resort
  Kona Village Luau/H
Lodge at Koele
  Lodge at Koele/Din. Rm./L
  Lodge at Koele/Terrace/L
Manago Hotel
  Manago Hotel/H
Manele Bay Hotel
  Manele Bay/Hulopo'e Ct./L
  Manele Bay/Ihilani/L
Marine Surf Hotel
  Matteo's
Maui Prince Hotel
  Hakone/M
  Prince Court/M
Mauna Kea Beach Hotel
  Batik/H
Mauna Lani Bay Hotel
  Bay Terrace/H
  Canoe House/H
Molokai Pizza Cafe
  Maunaloa Room/MO
New Otani Kaimana
  Hau Tree Lanai
Orchid at Mauna Lani
  Brown's Beach Hse./H
  Orchid Court/H
Outrigger Reef Hotel
  Shore Bird Bch. Broiler
Outrigger Waikiki
  Duke's Canoe Club
Pacific Beach Hotel
  Shogun
Plantation Inn
  Gerard's/M

Princeville Hotel
  Cafe Hanalei/K
  La Cascata/K
Renaissance Wailea
  Palm Court/M
Ritz-Carlton Hotel
  Anuenue Room/M
Royal Garden Hotel
  Cascada
Royal Hawaiian Hotel
  Surf Room
Sheraton Kauai Resort
  Shells/K
Sheraton Waikiki Hotel
  Hanohano Room
Waikiki Gateway Hotel
  Nick's Fishmarket
Waikiki Parc Hotel
  Parc Cafe
Waikiki Park Heights
  Hy's Steak Hse.
W Hotel
  Diamond Head Grill

"In" Places

Acqua
Alan Wong's
A Pacific Cafe
A Pacific Cafe/K
Bay Club/M
Beach House/K
Brew Moon
Cafe Pesto/H
Cascada
Chef Mavro's
Ciao Mein
Compadres
David Paul's Lahaina/M
Gerard's/M
Golden Dragon
Gordon Biersch
Haliimaile Gen. Store/M
Hau Tree Lanai
Henry Clay's Rotisserie/L
Indigo
Joe's B&G/M
Keo's
La Mer
Legend Seafood
Lodge at Koele/Dining Rm./L
Longhi's/M
Maha's Cafe/H
Mama's Fish House/M
Mariposa
Merriman's/H

Michel's
Nick's Fishmarket
Nick's Fishmarket/M
Oodles of Noodles/H
Orchids
Padovani's Bistro
Pahu i'a/H
Palomino
Piatti/K
Roussels/H
Roy's
Roy's Kahana B&G/M
Roy's Nicolina/M
Roy's Poipu B&G/K
Roy's Waikoloa B&G/H
Ruth's Chris/M
Sam Choy's Breakfast
Sam Choy's Diamond Head
Sansei Seafood/M
Seasons/M
Sunset Grill
Swiss Inn
3660 on the Rise

Jacket Required
Batik/H
La Mer
Lodge at Koele/Dining Rm./L

Late Late – After 12:30
(All hours are AM)
Aaron's Atop the Ala Moana (1)
Akasaka (2)
Eggs 'n Things (check hrs.)
Fook Yuen (3)
Ken's Hse. of Pancakes/H (24)
Kirin (2)
Panda Cuisine (2)
Royal Garden (2)
Ryan's Grill (1)
Wailana Coffee (24)
Yanagi Sushi (2)

Meet for a Drink
(Most top hotels and the
following standouts)
Angelo Pietro
Beach House/K
Brew Moon
Bull Shed/K
Cafe Pesto/H
Carelli's on the Beach/M
Chart House
Don Ho's
Duc's Bistro
Joe's Courtside Cafe/K

Longhi's/M
Murphy's B&G
Outback Steakhse.
Palomino
Plantation House/M
Roy's
Roy's Nicolina/M
Roy's Waikoloa B&G/H
Ruth's Chris/M
Ryan's Grill

Noteworthy Newcomers (10)
Aaron's Atop the Ala Moana
Diamond Head Grill
Feast at Lele/M
Hawaii Reg. Mktpl.
Joe's on the Green/K
Maunaloa Room/MO
OnJin's Cafe
Palm Cafe/H
Pineapple Room
Willows

Noteworthy Closings (24)
Aloha Cantina/M
Avalon/M
Bree Graden/H
Casa Donaldo
Cliquos
David Paul's Diamond Head Grill
Dynasty II
Fisherman's Gallery/K
Impromptu Café/M
Jamaican Cuisine Bar & Grill
Jean Marie's Pacific Bakery/K
Kaulapuu Cook House/M
K.K. Tei/H
Kola Broiler/K
Nicholas Nicholas
Nikko Japanese Steakhouse/M
Planet Hollywood/M
Rama Thai Restaurant
Sergio's
Shang Garden/K
Shark Tooth Steakhouse/M
Sun Sun Lau/H
Takanawa Sushi & Steakhse.
Ukuele Grill/M

Offbeat
Ahi's Punaluu
Aloha Cafe/H
A Saigon Cafe/M
Ba-Le French Sandwich
Bamboo/H

Brick Oven Pizza/K
Cafe Sistina
Chai's Island Bistro
Charley's/M
Contemporary Museum
Duane's Ono-Char/K
Hamura Saimin Stand/K
Hanapepe Cafe/K
Kakaako Kitchen
Kobe/M
Kua'Aina Sandwich
Little Bit of Saigon
Maha's Cafe/H
Ono Family Rest./K
Ono Hawaiian Foods
Sam Choy's Breakfast
Sam Sato's/M
Sibu Cafe/H
Tahiti Nui/K

Outdoor Dining
(G=garden; P=patio;
S=sidewalk; T=terrace;
W=waterside; best of many)
Aloha Cafe/H (T)
Bali-By-The-Sea (W)
Bay Club/M (P,W)
Bay Terrace/H (T)
Beach House/K (P,W)
Brown's Beach Hse./H (P,W)
Buzz's Wharf/M (W)
Cafe Hanalei/K (T)
Caffe Coco/K (G)
Canoe House/H (P,W)
Carelli's on the Beach/M (T,W)
Casa Di Amici/K (G,P,T)
Chai's Island Bistro (P)
Chart House/M (W)
Cheeseburger in Parad./M (W)
Coast Grille/H (T)
Compadres/M (P)
Contemporary Museum (G,P)
Dixie Grill BBQ (P)
Donatoni's/H (W)
Dondero's/K (P)
Don Ho's (P,W)
Duane's Ono-Char/K (P)
Duke's Canoe Club (P)
Duke's Canoe Club/K (P)
Edward's at Kanaloa/H (T,W)
Ferraro's at Seaside/M (G)
Gaylord's at Kilohana/K (G,P)
Gerard's/M (T)
Gordon Biersch (P,W)
Greek Bistro/M (G,W)

Hanamaulu/K (G)
Hard Rock Cafe/H (P)
Harrington's/H (W)
Hau Tree Lanai (P,W)
Hualalai Club Grille/H (P)
Huggo's/H (P,W)
Hula Grill/M (P,W)
Ilima Terrace/K (T,W)
I Love Country Cafe (S)
Indigo (G,P,T)
i'o/M (G,P,W)
Jacques on the Beach/M (G)
Jameson's by the Sea/H (P,T,W)
JJ's Broiler/K (P,W)
Joe's Courtside Cafe/K (T)
Joe's on the Green/K (T)
John Dominis (W)
Kamuela Provision Co./H (P,W)
Kawaihae Harbor Grill/H (T)
Kea Lani/M (P,T)
Keoki's Paradise/K (P)
Kimo's/M (P,W)
Kona Inn/H (T,W)
Kua'Aina Sandwich (P,S)
Kula Lodge/M (G,T)
Lahaina Coolers/M (P)
La Mer (T,W)
Leilani's on the Beach/M (P,T,W)
Mama's Fish House/M (W)
Manele Bay/Hulopo'e Court/L (T)
Manele Bay/Ihilani/L (T)
Michel's (W)
Milagros Food Co./M (S)
Nick's Fishmarket/M (P)
Ninon/H (W)
Olive Tree Cafe (P,S)
OnJin's Cafe (S)
Orchid Court/H (T)
Orchids (T,W)
pacific'O/M (G,P,T,W)
Pahu i'a/H (W)
Palm Court/M (T)
Piatti/K (P)
Pioneer Inn/M (P)
Plantation Hse. of Poipu/K (P)
Postcards Cafe/K (P)
Roy's Poipu B&G/K (S)
Roy's Waikoloa B&G/H (P,W)
Scoozee's (P)
Seaside/H (P,W)
Seasons/M (T)
Shells/K (T,W)
Shore Bird Bch. Broiler (P,W)
Sibu Cafe/H (P)
Singha Thai (G)

Surf Room (W)
Tahiti Nui/K (P)
Tidepools/K (W)
Tomkats Grille/K (P)
Trattoria (T)
Wailua Marina/K (P,T,W)
Waterfront/M (P,W)
Whalers Brewpub/K (P,T)
Willows (G,P)

Outstanding Views
Aloha Cafe/H
Bali-By-The-Sea
Batik/H
Bay Club/M
Beach House/K
Brennecke's Bch. Broiler/K
Brown's Beach Hse./H
Buzz's Wharf/M
Cafe Hanalei/K
Canoe House/H
Carelli's on the Beach/M
Coast Grille/H
Edward's at Kanaloa/H
Ferraro's at Seaside/M
Gordon Biersch
Hanohano Room
Hau Tree Lanai
Hoku's
Huggo's/H
Hula Grill/M
Ilima Terrace/K
i'o/M
Jameson's by the Sea/H
John Dominis
Kimo's/M
Kula Lodge/M
La Mer
Leilani's on the Beach/M
Mama's Fish House/M
Manele Bay/Hulopo'e Court/L
Mariposa
Michel's
Naupaka Terrace
Nick's Fishmarket/M
Ohia Lodge/MO
Old Lahaina Luau/M
Orchids
Pacific Grill/M
pacific'O/M
Pahu i'a/H
Plantation House/M
Plumeria Beach Cafe
Sarento's Top of the I
Seasons/M

Seawatch/M
Shells/K
Shore Bird Bch. Broiler
Surf Room
Swan Court/M
Tidepools/K
Waterfront/M

Parties & Private Rooms
(Any nightclub or restaurant
charges less at off-times;
* indicates private rooms
available; best of many)
Aaron's Atop the Ala Moana*
Acqua
Akasaka
Alfred's*
Anuenue Room/M*
A Pacific Cafe
A Pacific Cafe/K*
A Pacific Cafe/M
Azul*
Bali-By-The-Sea
Bamboo/H
Bay Terrace/H
Benihana*
Brew Moon
Buzz's Original Steakhse.
Buzz's Wharf/M
Cafe Che Pasta
Cafe Portofino/K
Casa Di Amici/K*
Cascada
Chai's Island Bistro
China House
Ciao Mein
David Paul's Lahaina/M
Diamond Head Grill*
Donatoni's/H*
Donato's
Dondero's/K
Duke's Canoe Club*
Duke's Canoe Club/K*
Eastern Garden
Fiascos/H*
Gaylord's at Kilohana/K
Gerard's/M
Golden Dragon*
Haliimaile Gen. Store/M
Hee Hing
Hula Grill/M
Hy's Steak Hse.
Ilima Terrace/K
Joe's on the Green/K
John Dominis*

Kyo-Ya
La Cascata/K
La Mer
Legend Seafood
L'Uraku
Matteo's
Michel's*
Nick's Fishmarket
Nick's Fishmarket/M
Ninon/H
Oodles of Noodles/H
Orchid Court/H
Orchids
Outback Steakhse./M
Piatti/K*
Pineapple Room
Plantation House/M
Plumeria Beach Cafe
Postcards Cafe/K
Prince Court/M*
Prince Court Rest.*
Rest. Suntory*
Royal Garden
Royal Siam/H
Roy's
Roy's Kahana B&G/M
Roy's Poipu B&G/K
Roy's Waikoloa B&G/H
Ruth's Chris/M
Sam Choy's Breakfast
Sarento's Top of the I*
Seaside/H
Seasons/M*
Seawatch/M
Shells/K*
Shogun
Singha Thai
Sunset Grill
Tai-Pan on the Blvd.
Tanaka of Tokyo
Teshima/H*
Tidepools/K
Tony Roma's
Trattoria
Tres Hombres/H
Verbano
Wailua Marina/K*
Waimea Brewing Co./K*
Wasabi Bistro
Whalers Brewpub/K

People-Watching
Acqua
A Pacific Cafe
Assaggio

Bali-By-The-Sea
Bay Club/M
Brennecke's Bch. Broiler/K
Brew Moon
Brown's Beach Hse./H
Cafe Che Pasta
Cafe Pesto/H
Cafe Portofino/K
California Pizza Kitchen
Charley's/M
Compadres
Donatoni's/H
Don Ho's
Gordon Biersch
Hau Tree Lanai
Hoku's
Huggo's/H
Hula Grill/M
Indigo
Jameson's by the Sea/H
Joe's B&G/M
Keo's
La Mer
Leilani's on the Beach/M
Longhi's/M
Mama's Fish House/M
Manele Bay/Ihilani/L
Mariposa
Merriman's/H
Michel's
Mocha Java
Murphy's B&G
Nick's Fishmarket
Nick's Fishmarket/M
Oodles of Noodles/H
Orchids
Padovani's Bistro
Pahu i'a/H
Palm Court/M
Roy's
Roy's Kahana B&G/M
Roy's Nicolina/M
Ryan's Grill
Sam Choy's Breakfast
Sansei Seafood/M
Sarento's Top of the I
Seasons/M
Sibu Cafe/H
Sunset Grill

Power Scenes
A Pacific Cafe
Chef Mavro's
David Paul's Lahaina/M
Eastern Garden

Kyo-Ya
La Mer
Merriman's/H
Michel's
Pahu i'a/H
Roy's Kahana B&G/M
Ruth's Chris/M
Seasons/M
Waterfront/M

Prix Fixe Menus
(Call to check prices,
days and times)
Acqua
Akasaka
Anuenue Room/M
A Pacific Cafe/M
Azul
Ba-Le French Sandwich
Bali-By-The-Sea
Beau Soleil
Boston's North End Pizza
Buzz's Original Steakhse.
Ciao Mein
Coast Grille/H
Duc's Bistro
Feast at Lele/M
Golden Dragon
Hale Vietnam
Hanohano Room
Hoku's
Kyo-Ya
La Cascata/K
La Mer
L'Uraku
Manele Bay/Ihilani/L
Mini Garden
Nick's Fishmarket
Nick's Fishmarket/M
Orchid Court/H
Orchids
Paesano
Panda Cuisine
Patisserie
Princo Court/M
Prince Court Rest.
Roy's Nicolina/M
Roy's Waikoloa B&G/H
Ruth's Chris
Seasons/M
Singha Thai
Surf Room
Swan Court/M
Tai-Pan on the Blvd.
Willows

Pubs/Bars/Microbreweries
Brew Moon
Dixie Grill BBQ
Gordon Biersch
Murphy's B&G
Outback Steakhse.
Sam Choy's Breakfast
Whalers Brewpub/K

Quiet Conversation
Alfred's
Anuenue Room/M
Baci Bistro
Batik/H
Beau Soleil
Canoe House/H
Cascada
Coast Grille/H
Contemporary Museum
Dondero's/K
Gerard's/M
Hakone
Hakone/H
Hau Tree Lanai
Ilima Terrace/K
Indigo
Kalaheo Steak Hse./K
Keo's
Kirin
Kona Ranch Hse./H
Kyotaru Hawaii
La Mer
Mama's Fish House/M
Manele Bay/Hulopo'e Court/L
Manele Bay/Ihilani/L
Merriman's/H
Michel's
Naupaka Terrace
Orchids
Paesano
Prince Court/M
Ruth's Chris
Ruth's Chris/M
Sarento's Top of the I
Singha Thai
Tanaka of Tokyo
Tokyo Tei/M
Trattoria
Verbano
Village Grill/MO

Reservations Essential
Aaron's Atop the Ala Moana
Acqua
Alan Wong's

Azul
Baci Bistro
Bali-By-The-Sea
Batik/H
Bay Club/M
Bay Terrace/H
Beau Soleil
Brown's Beach Hse./H
Canoe House/H
Coast Grille/H
Donatoni's/H
Edward's at Kanaloa/H
Hakone
Hakone/H
Hakone/M
Hanohano Room
Hoku's
Kona Village Luau/H
La Cascata/K
Lodge at Koele/Dining Rm./L
Mama's Fish House/M
Manele Bay/Ihilani/L
Mariposa
Merriman's/H
Michel's
Nick's Fishmarket/M
Pahu i'a/H
Pescatore/H
Plantation House/M
Postcards Cafe/K
Pyramids
Roy's Kahana B&G/M
Roy's Waikoloa B&G/H
Sam Choy's Diamond Head
Singha Thai
Surf Room
Swiss Inn

Romantic Spots

Alfred's
Anuenue Room/M
Azul
Bali-By-The-Sea
Batik/H
Bay Club/M
Beach House/K
Canoe House/H
Cascada
Chai's Island Bistro
Chart House
Chart House/M
Chef Mavro's
Chez Paul/M
Coast Grille/H
Donatoni's/H

Dondero's/K
Duc's Bistro
Edward's at Kanaloa/H
Ferraro's at Seaside/M
Gerard's/M
Hanohano Room
Harrington's/H
Hau Tree Lanai
Huggo's/H
Hula Grill/M
Jameson's by the Sea/H
Kilauea Lodge/H
Kula Lodge/M
La Cascata/K
La Mer
Leilani's on the Beach/M
Lodge at Koele/Dining Rm./L
Mama's Fish House/M
Manele Bay/Hulopo'e Court/L
Manele Bay/Ihilani/L
Mariposa
Michel's
Naupaka Terrace
Nick's Fishmarket/M
Orchids
pacific'O/M
Padovani's Bistro
Pahu i'a/H
Palm Court/M
Piatti/K
Plantation House/M
Prince Court/M
Royal Garden
Roy's Waikoloa B&G/H
Sam Choy's Diamond Head
Sarento's Top of the I
Seasons/M
Shells/K
Surf Room
Swan Court/M
Tidepools/K
Waterfront/M

Saturday – Best Bets
(B=brunch; L=lunch;
best of many)
Ahi's Punaluu (L)
Aloha Cafe/H (L)
Angelo Pietro (L)
A Saigon Cafe/M (L)
Assaggio (L)
Azteca (L)
Bamboo/H (L)
Bay Club/M (L)
Big Island Steak Hse. (L)

Brennecke's Bch. Broiler/K (L)
Brew Moon (L)
Brick Oven Pizza/K (L)
Buzz's Wharf/M (L)
Cafe Haleiwa (L)
Cafe Pesto/H (L)
Caffe Coco/K (L)
California Pizza Kitchen (L)
Charley's/M (L)
Ciao Mein (L)
Compadres (L)
Diamond Head Grill (L)
Don Ho's (B,L)
Don's Grill/H (L)
Edelweiss/H (L)
Edward's at Kanaloa/H (L)
Fiascos/H (L)
Gaylord's at Kilohana/K (L)
Green Garden/K (L)
Hula Grill/M (L)
Ilima Terrace/K (L)
Jameson's by the Sea/M (L)
JJ's Broiler/K (L)
Joe's Courtside Cafe/K (L)
Joe's on the Green/K (L)
Kakaako Kitchen (L)
Kawaihae Harbor Grill/H (L)
Keoki's Paradise/K (L)
Kimo's/M (L)
Kincaid's (L)
Koa Hse. Grill/H (L)
Kona Inn/H (L)
Kona Ranch Hse./H (B,L)
Kyo-Ya (L)
Leilani's on the Beach/M (L)
Little Bit of Saigon (L)
Longhi's/M (L)
Mama's Fish House/M (L)
Maple Garden (L)
Mariposa (L)
Mocha Java (B,L)
Murphy's B&G (L)
Naupaka Terrace (L)
Olive Tree Cafe (L)
Ono Hawaiian Foods (L)
Oodles of Noodles/H (L)
Orchids (L)
pacific'O/M (L)
Padovani's Bistro (L)
Paesano (L)
Paia Fishmarket/M (L)
Paniolo Country Inn/H (L)
Parc Cafe (L)
Pescatore/H (L)
Pineapple Room (L)

Plantation House/M (L)
Plantation Hse. of Poipu/K (L)
Plumeria Beach Cafe (L)
Quinn's/H (L)
Roy's Waikoloa B&G/H (L)
Sam Choy's Breakfast (L)
Sam Choy's Kahului/M (L)
Scoozee's (L)
Seawatch/M (L)
Surt's at Volcano Village/H (L)
Teshima/H (L)
Tomkats Grille/K (L)
Tony Roma's (L)
Tony Roma's/M (L)
Tres Hombres/H (L)
Verbano (L)
Wailua Marina/K (L)
Waimea Brewing Co./K (L)
Wasabi Bistro (L)
Whalers Brewpub/K (L)
Willows (L)
Zelo's Beach Hse./K (L)

Sunday – Best Bets
(B=brunch; L=lunch;
D=dinner; plus all hotels
and most Asians)
Aloha Cafe/H (B,L)
Angelo Pietro (L,D)
Assaggio (L,D)
Bamboo/H (B)
Bay Club/M (L,D)
Bay Terrace/H (B)
Big City Diner - Kaimuki (B,L,D)
Big Island Steak Hse. (L,D)
Brennecke's Bch. Broiler/K (L,D)
Brew Moon (B,L,D)
Buzz's Wharf/M (L,D)
Cafe Haleiwa (B,L)
Cafe Pesto/H (L,D)
Caffe Coco/K (B,L,D)
California Pizza Kitchen (L,D)
Camp Hse. Grill/K (L,D)
Casanova/M (L,D)
Chai's Island Bistro (L,D)
Charley's/M (L,D)
Ciao Mein (L,D)
Compadres (L,D)
Diamond Head Grill (L,D)
Don Ho's (B,L,D)
Don's Grill/H (L,D)
Edward's at Kanaloa/H (L,D)
Eggbert's/K (L,D)
Ferraro's at Seaside/M (L,D)
Fiascos/H (L,D)

Gaylord's at Kilohana/K (B,D)
Green Garden/K (L,D)
Haliimaile Gen. Store/M (B,L,D)
Hanohano Room (B,D)
Hula Grill/M (L,D)
Ilima Terrace/K (B,L,D)
Jameson's by the Sea/M (L,D)
JJ's Broiler/K (L,D)
Joe's Courtside Cafe/K (L)
Joe's on the Green/K (L)
John Dominis (B,D)
Kawaihae Harbor Grill/H (L,D)
Keoki's Paradise/K (L,D)
Kimo's/M (L,D)
Kincaid's (L,D)
Koa Hse. Grill/H (B,L,D)
Kona Inn/H (L,D)
Kona Ranch Hse./H (B,L)
Kua'Aina Sandwich (L,D)
Lahaina Coolers/M (L,D)
Leilani's on the Beach/M (L,D)
Longhi's/M (L,D)
L'Uraku (L,D)
Maha's Cafe/H (L)
Mama's Fish House/M (L,D)
Maple Garden (L,D)
Mariposa (L,D)
Milagros Food Co./M (L,D)
Mini Garden (L,D)
Mocha Java (B,L,D)
Naupaka Terrace (B,L,D)
Olive Tree Cafe (L,D)
Ono Family Rest./K (L)
Ono Hawaiian Foods (L,D)
Oodles of Noodles/H (L,D)
pacific'O/M (L,D)
Padovani's Bistro (L,D)
Paia Fishmarket/M (L,D)
Paniolo Country Inn/H (L,D)
Parc Cafe (B,D)
Pescatore/H (L,D)
Pineapple Room (B,L,D)
Plantation House/M (L,D)
Plantation Hse. of Poipu/K (L,D)
Postcards Cafe/K (B,D)
Quinn's/H (L,D)
Roy's Waikoloa B&G/H (L,D)
Ryan's Grill (B,L,D)
Sam Choy's Breakfast (L,D)
Sam Choy's Diam. Head (B,D)
Seawatch/M (L,D)
Sibu Cafe/H (L,D)
Surf Room (B,L,D)
Surt's at Volcano Village/H (L,D)
Swiss Inn (B,D)

Tomkats Grille/K (L,D)
Tony Roma's (L,D)
Tony Roma's/M (L,D)
Tres Hombres/H (L,D)
Verbano (L,D)
Wailua Marina/K (L,D)
Waimea Brewing Co./K (L,D)
Waterfront/M (L,D)
Whalers Brewpub/K (L,D)
Willows (L,D)
Zelo's Beach Hse./K (L,D)

Senior Appeal
Assaggio
Bamboo/H
Brick Oven Pizza/K
Don Ho's
Don's Grill/H
Eastern Garden
Gaylord's at Kilohana/K
Hula Grill/M
Joe's Courtside Cafe/K
Joe's on the Green/K
Kakaako Kitchen
Kalaheo Steak Hse./K
Keo's
Kincaid's
Kona Ranch Hse./H
Manele Bay/Hulopo'e Court/L
Manele Bay/Ihilani/L
Mariposa
Mekong Thai
Mema Thai Chinese/K
Naupaka Terrace
OnJin's Cafe
Ono Family Rest./K
Oodles of Noodles/H
Orchids
Paesano
Palm Court/M
Patisserie
Plantation House/M
Ruth's Chris/M
Singha Thai
3660 on the Rise
Tony Roma's
Verbano
Village Grill/MO
Wailana Coffee
Yohei Sushi

Singles Scenes
Boston's North End Pizza
Brew Moon
Bubba Burgers/K
Cafe Haleiwa

Cafe Portofino/K
California Bch. Rock n' Sushi
California Pizza Kitchen
Casa Di Amici/K
Charley's/M
Cheeseburger in Paradise
Cheeseburger in Paradise/M
Compadres
Dixie Grill BBQ
Duke's Canoe Club
Duke's Canoe Club/K
Gordon Biersch
Huggo's/H
Hula Grill/M
JJ's Broiler/K
Keo's
Leilani's on the Beach/M
Outback Steakhse.
Ryan's Grill
Sarento's Top of the I

Sleepers
(Good to excellent food,
but little known)
Aloha Cafe/H
Cafe Haleiwa
Caffe Coco/K
Coffee Gallery
Hanalei Wake-Up/K
Kakaako Kitchen
Keei Cafe/H
Lahaina Coolers/M
Maha's Cafe/H
Milagros Food Co./M
Mocha Java
Pauwela Cafe/M
Postcards Cafe/K
Quinn's/H
Roadrunner Bakery/K

Teflons
(Get lots of business, despite
so-so food, i.e. they have
other attractions that prevent
criticism from sticking)
Ahi's Punaluu
Auntie Pasto's
Big City Diner - Kaimuki
Cheeseburger in Paradise
Cheeseburger in Paradise/M
Chowder House
Compadres
Duke's Canoe Club
Duke's Canoe Club/K
Fiascos/H

Grace's Drive Inn
Hard Rock Cafe
Hard Rock Cafe/H
Hard Rock Cafe/M
Ken's Hse. of Pancakes/H
Kokee Lodge/K
Murphy's B&G
Ocean View Inn/H
Pioneer Inn/M
Shore Bird Bch. Broiler
Wailana Coffee

Teenagers & Other Youthful Spirits
Auntie Pasto's
Ba-Le French Sandwich
Bianelli's Pizza/H
Boston's North End Pizza
Bubba Burgers/K
Cafe Haleiwa
California Bch. Rock n' Sushi
California Pizza Kitchen
Cheeseburger in Paradise
Cheeseburger in Paradise/M
Dixie Grill BBQ
Duane's Ono-Char/K
Fiascos/H
Hard Rock Cafe
Hard Rock Cafe/H
Hard Rock Cafe/M
Harpo's Pizza
Hula Grill/M
Keoki's Paradise/K
Kua'Aina Sandwich
Leilani's on the Beach/M
Maui Tacos
Maui Tacos/H
Maui Tacos/M
Molokai Pizza Cafe/MO
Polli's/M
Sansei Seafood/M
Scoozee's

Valet Parking
Aaron's Atop the Ala Moana
Acqua
Alan Wong's
Alfred's
Angelo Pietro
Anuenue Room/M
Assaggio
Azul
Bali-By-The-Sea
Bay Terrace/H
Beach House/K

Brew Moon
Brown's Beach Hse./H
Cafe Hanalei/K
California Pizza Kitchen
Carelli's on the Beach/M
Cascada
Chai's Island Bistro
Chef Mavro's
Ciao Mein
Diamond Head Grill
Dixie Grill BBQ
Donatoni's/H
Donato's
Dondero's/K
Don Ho's
Duke's Canoe Club
Duke's Canoe Club/K
Ferraro's at Seaside/M
Gaylord's at Kilohana/K
Golden Dragon
Gordon Biersch
Hakone
Hakone/H
Hakone/M
Hanohano Room
Hard Rock Cafe/H
Hau Tree Lanai
Hee Hing
Hoku's
Hualalai Club Grille/H
Huggo's/H
Hy's Steak Hse.
Ilima Terrace/K
Indigo
Joe's Courtside Cafe/K
John Dominis
Keo's
Kobe
Kyo-Ya
La Cascata/K
La Mer
L'Uraku
Manago Hotel/H
Manele Bay/Ihilani/L
Maple Garden
Mariposa
Michel's
Naupaka Terrace
Nick's Fishmarket
Nick's Fishmarket/M
Ninniku-Ya Garlic
Orchid Court/H
Orchids
Pacific Grill/M
Paesano

Palm Court/M
Palomino
Parc Cafe
Plumeria Beach Cafe
Prince Court/M
Ryan's Grill
Sam Choy's Breakfast
Sam Choy's Diamond Head
Sarento's Top of the I
Seasons/M
Seawatch/M
Shells/K
Shogun
Surf Room
Swan Court/M
Tai-Pan on the Blvd.
3660 on the Rise
Tidepools/K
Tony Roma's
Tony Roma's/M
Trattoria
Wasabi Bistro
Waterfront/M
Whalers Brewpub/K
Won Kee
Yanagi Sushi
Yohei Sushi

Visitors on Expense Accounts
Acqua
Alan Wong's
Anuenue Room/M
A Pacific Cafe/K
A Pacific Cafe/M
Azul
Bali-By-The-Sea
Batik/H
Bay Terrace/H
Beach House/K
Benihana
Cafe Hanalei/K
Chart House/M
Chef Mavro's
Chez Paul/M
Coast Grille/H
David Paul's Lahaina/M
Donatoni's/H
Dondero's/K
Edward's at Kanaloa/H
Ferraro's at Seaside/M
Golden Dragon
Hakone
Hakone/M
Haliimaile Gen. Store/M

Hanohano Room
Joe's B&G/M
John Dominis
La Cascata/K
Legend Seafood
Longhi's/M
Manele Bay/Hulopo'e Court/L
Manele Bay/Ihilani/L
Merriman's/H
Michel's
Nick's Fishmarket
Nick's Fishmarket/M
Orchids
Pacific Grill/M
Pahu i'a/H
Prince Court/M
Prince Court Rest.
Rest. Kintaro/K
Roy's
Roy's Kahana B&G/M
Roy's Nicolina/M
Roy's Waikoloa B&G/H
Ruth's Chris
Ruth's Chris/M
Sam Choy's Diamond Head
Sarento's Top of the I
Seasons/M
Shogun
Sunset Grill
Tanaka of Tokyo
3660 on the Rise

Wheelchair Access
(Most places now have wheelchair access; call in advance to check)

Wine/Beer Only
Ahi's Punaluu
Akasaka
Aloha Cafe/H
Angelo Pietro
Auntie Pasto's
Bali-By-The-Sea
Brick Oven Pizza/K
Cafe Monsarrat
Cafe Pesto/H
California Bch. Rock n' Sushi
Camp Hse. Grill/K
Don's Grill/H
Kalaheo Steak Hse./K
Keei Cafe/H
Kyotaru Hawaii
Mekong Thai
Mocha Java

OnJin's Cafe
Paia Fishmarket/M
Postcards Cafe/K
Royal Siam/H
Seaside/H
Sibu Cafe/H
Stella Blues/M
Surt's at Volcano Village/H
Yohei Sushi

Winning Wine Lists
Alan Wong's
Anuenue Room/M
Azul
Bali-By-The-Sea
Batik/H
Bay Club/M
Cascada
Chef Mavro's
Gerard's/M
Joe's B&G/M
La Cascata/K
La Mer
Longhi's/M
Manele Bay/Hulopo'e Court/L
Manele Bay/Ihilani/L
Mariposa
Matteo's
Michel's
Naupaka Terrace
Nick's Fishmarket
Orchids
Padovani's Bistro
Pahu i'a/H
Prince Court Rest.
Ruth's Chris/M
Sarento's Top of the I
Sunset Grill
Trattoria
Waterfront/M

Young Children
(Besides the normal fast-food places; * indicates children's menu available)
Aaron's Atop the Ala Moana*
Acqua*
Angelo Pietro*
A Pacific Cafe*
A Pacific Cafe/M*
Azteca
Beach House/K*
Big City Diner - Kaimuki*
Big Island Steak Hse.*
Big Island Steak Hse./H*

Brennecke's Bch. Broiler/K*
Brick Oven Pizza/K
Bubba Gump Shrimp
Buzz's Wharf/M*
Cafe Hanalei/K*
Cafe Pesto/H*
Cafe Portofino/K*
California Pizza Kitchen
Camp Hse. Grill/K*
Chowder House*
Compadres*
Dixie Grill BBQ*
Don's Grill/H*
Duane's Ono-Char/K*
Duke's Canoe Club*
Duke's Canoe Club/K*
Eggbert's/K*
Eggs 'n Things
Fiascos/H*
Green Garden/K*
Hard Rock Cafe*
Harpo's Pizza*
Huggo's/H
Hula Grill/M
I Love Country Cafe*
Jacques on the Beach/M*
JJ's Broiler/K
Joe's on the Green/K*
Kalaheo Coffee/K*
Kamuela Provision Co./H*
Kawaihae Harbor Grill/H*
Ken's Hse. of Pancakes/H*
Keoki's Paradise/K*

Kimo's/M*
Kincaid's*
Kona Inn/H*
Kona Ranch Hse./H*
Lahaina Coolers/M*
Leilani's on the Beach/M*
Lodge at Koele/Dining Rm./L*
Mama's Fish House/M
Maui Tacos*
Maui Tacos/H*
Maui Tacos/M
Molokai Pizza Cafe/MO*
Ono Family Rest./K*
Oodles of Noodles/H*
Outback Steakhse.*
Outback Steakhse./M*
Palomino*
Pauwela Cafe/M*
Pioneer Inn/M
Plantation Hse. of Poipu/K*
Plumeria Beach Cafe*
Quinn's/H*
Roadrunner Bakery/K*
Ryan's Grill*
Sam Choy's Breakfast*
Seawatch/M*
Shells/K*
Shore Bird Bch. Broiler*
Stella Blues/M*
Tomkats Grille/K*
Tony Roma's
Tres Hombres/H*
Wailana Coffee

ALPHABETICAL PAGE INDEX

112   www.zagat.com

Rating Sheets

To aid in your participation in our next *Survey*

	F	**D**	**S**	**C**

⌐⌐⌐⌐

Restaurant Name _____
Phone _____
Comments _____
_____
_____

⌐⌐⌐⌐

Restaurant Name _____
Phone _____
Comments _____
_____
_____

⌐⌐⌐⌐

Restaurant Name _____
Phone _____
Comments _____
_____
_____

⌐⌐⌐⌐

Restaurant Name _____
Phone _____
Comments _____
_____
_____

⌐⌐⌐⌐

Restaurant Name _____
Phone _____
Comments _____
_____
_____

⌐⌐⌐⌐

Restaurant Name _____
Phone _____
Comments _____
_____
_____

	F	D	S	C

⌐⌐⌐⌐

Restaurant Name _____
Phone _____
Comments _____
_____
_____

⌐⌐⌐⌐

Restaurant Name _____
Phone _____
Comments _____
_____
_____

⌐⌐⌐⌐

Restaurant Name _____
Phone _____
Comments _____
_____
_____

⌐⌐⌐⌐

Restaurant Name _____
Phone _____
Comments _____
_____
_____

⌐⌐⌐⌐

Restaurant Name _____
Phone _____
Comments _____
_____
_____

⌐⌐⌐⌐

Restaurant Name _____
Phone _____
Comments _____
_____
_____

	F	D	S	C

⌐⌐⌐⌐

Restaurant Name _____
Phone _____
Comments _____
_____
_____

⌐⌐⌐⌐

Restaurant Name _____
Phone _____
Comments _____
_____
_____

⌐⌐⌐⌐

Restaurant Name _____
Phone _____
Comments _____
_____
_____

⌐⌐⌐⌐

Restaurant Name _____
Phone _____
Comments _____
_____
_____

⌐⌐⌐⌐

Restaurant Name _____
Phone _____
Comments _____
_____
_____

⌐⌐⌐⌐

Restaurant Name _____
Phone _____
Comments _____
_____
_____

	F	D	S	C

⌐⌐⌐⌐

Restaurant Name _____
Phone _____
Comments _____
_____
_____

⌐⌐⌐⌐

Restaurant Name _____
Phone _____
Comments _____
_____
_____

⌐⌐⌐⌐

Restaurant Name _____
Phone _____
Comments _____
_____
_____

⌐⌐⌐⌐

Restaurant Name _____
Phone _____
Comments _____
_____
_____

⌐⌐⌐⌐

Restaurant Name _____
Phone _____
Comments _____
_____
_____

⌐⌐⌐⌐

Restaurant Name _____
Phone _____
Comments _____
_____
_____

	F	D	S	C

⌐ ⌐ ⌐ ⌐

Restaurant Name _____
Phone _____
Comments _____
_____
_____

⌐ ⌐ ⌐ ⌐

Restaurant Name _____
Phone _____
Comments _____
_____
_____

⌐ ⌐ ⌐ ⌐

Restaurant Name _____
Phone _____
Comments _____
_____
_____

⌐ ⌐ ⌐ ⌐

Restaurant Name _____
Phone _____
Comments _____
_____
_____

⌐ ⌐ ⌐ ⌐

Restaurant Name _____
Phone _____
Comments _____
_____
_____

⌐ ⌐ ⌐ ⌐

Restaurant Name _____
Phone _____
Comments _____
_____
_____

⌐⌐⌐⌐

Restaurant Name _____
Phone _____
Comments _____
_____
_____

⌐⌐⌐⌐

Restaurant Name _____
Phone _____
Comments _____
_____
_____

⌐⌐⌐⌐

Restaurant Name _____
Phone _____
Comments _____
_____
_____

⌐⌐⌐⌐

Restaurant Name _____
Phone _____
Comments _____
_____
_____

⌐⌐⌐⌐

Restaurant Name _____
Phone _____
Comments _____
_____
_____

⌐⌐⌐⌐

Restaurant Name _____
Phone _____
Comments _____
_____
_____

	F	D	S	C

⌐⌐⌐⌐

Restaurant Name _____
Phone _____
Comments _____
_____
_____

⌐⌐⌐⌐

Restaurant Name _____
Phone _____
Comments _____
_____
_____

⌐⌐⌐⌐

Restaurant Name _____
Phone _____
Comments _____
_____
_____

⌐⌐⌐⌐

Restaurant Name _____
Phone _____
Comments _____
_____
_____

⌐⌐⌐⌐

Restaurant Name _____
Phone _____
Comments _____
_____
_____

⌐⌐⌐⌐

Restaurant Name _____
Phone _____
Comments _____
_____
_____

| | **F** | **D** | **S** | **C** |

⌐⌐⌐⌐

Restaurant Name _____
Phone _____
Comments _____
_____
_____

⌐⌐⌐⌐

Restaurant Name _____
Phone _____
Comments _____
_____
_____

⌐⌐⌐⌐

Restaurant Name _____
Phone _____
Comments _____
_____
_____

⌐⌐⌐⌐

Restaurant Name _____
Phone _____
Comments _____
_____
_____

⌐⌐⌐⌐

Restaurant Name _____
Phone _____
Comments _____
_____
_____

⌐⌐⌐⌐

Restaurant Name _____
Phone _____
Comments _____
_____
_____

Wine Vintage Chart 1985-1998

This chart is designed to help you select wine to go with your meal. It is based on the same 0 to 30 scale used throughout this *Survey*. The ratings (prepared by our friend **Howard Stravitz**, a law professor at the University of South Carolina) reflect both the quality of the vintage and the wine's readiness for present consumption. Thus, if a wine is not fully mature or is over the hill, its rating has been reduced. We do not include 1987, 1991 or 1993 vintages because, with the exception of cabernets, '91 Northern Rhônes and '93 red Burgundies and Southern Rhônes, those vintages are not especially recommended.

	'85	'86	'88	'89	'90	'92	'94	'95	'96	'97	'98
WHITES											
French:											
Alsace	25	20	23	28	28	24	28	26	24	25	24
Burgundy	24	25	19	27	22	23	22	27	28	25	24
Loire Valley	–	–	–	26	25	18	22	24	26	23	22
Champagne	28	25	24	26	28	–	–	24	26	24	–
Sauternes	22	28	29	25	26	–	18	22	23	24	–
California:											
Chardonnay	–	–	–	–	–	24	22	26	22	26	26
REDS											
French:											
Bordeaux	26	27	25	28	29	18	24	25	24	23	23
Burgundy	24	–	23	27	29	23	23	25	26	24	24
Rhône	26	20	26	28	27	15	23	24	22	24	26
Beaujolais	–	–	–	–	–	–	21	24	22	24	23
California:											
Cab./Merlot	26	26	–	21	28	26	27	25	24	25	26
Zinfandel	–	–	–	–	–	21	23	21	22	24	25
Italian:											
Tuscany	27	–	24	–	26	–	–	25	19	28	25
Piedmont	25	–	25	27	27	–	–	23	25	28	25

Bargain sippers take note: Some wines are reliable year in, year out, and are reasonably priced as well. They include: Alsatian Pinot Blancs, Côtes du Rhône, Muscadet, Bardolino, Valpolicella and inexpensive Spanish Rioja and California Zinfandel and are best bought in the most recent vintages.

May We Quote You?

Be a part of
ZAGAT SURVEY®

If you would like to participate in one of our Surveys or be added to our mailing list, please fill out this card and send it back to us.

☐ Mr. ☐ Mrs. ☐ Ms.

_____
Your Name

_____
Street Address   Apt #

_____
City   State   Zip

_____
e-mail Address

_____
Occupation

I'd like to be a surveyor for the following city:

_____

or a surveyor for U.S. Hotels, Resorts & Spas ☐

The city I visit most is: ——————————————

My favorite restaurant is: ——————————————

                              ——————————————
                                    City

My favorite hotel is: ——————————————

                              ——————————————
                                    City

I eat roughly ——— lunches and dinners out per week.

☐ This book was a gift ☐ Bought by me ☐ Surveyor copy

The title of this book is: ——————————————